HOPES AND FEARS

Australian Migration Stories

CELEBRATING

NATIONAL LIBRARY
OF AUSTRALIA
PUBLISHING

OVER 50 YEARS

JOE GREENBERG (1923–2007) *Australia: Land of Tomorrow*, c. 1948

FOREWORD

The National Library of Australia's collections reflect the cultural diversity of the Australian people, and they are all the richer because of this. We actively seek collection material from culturally and linguistically diverse sections of our community, including Australians with Indian heritage through this year's Indian Diaspora in Australia Collecting Project.

In personal papers and photograph albums, published family histories and ephemera, millions of Australian stories are made available for interpretation or enjoyment. A common theme in these stories is migration, whether it occurred with the early days of British settlement or at any other point in our nation's recent history. Some of this migration was hope-filled and voluntary— the 22 year-old Kwong Sue Duk migrating to Cooktown, Queensland, to seek his fortune on the goldfields in 1875, or the family joining their compatriots in the fourth most populous 'Greek' city, Melbourne, in 1975. Some was not— Fatah and Makai Mohmand who arrived as refugees in Melbourne having fled Afghanistan after the invasion by the Soviet Union, or Kwirina who escaped ethnic conflict in Burundi after eight years in a Tanzanian refugee camp and who now calls Blacktown, New South Wales, home.

This book is a companion to the National Library of Australia's exhibition *Hopes and Fears: Australian Migration Stories*. The exhibition tells these stories, and more, to present a kaleidoscope of historical and contemporary migrant experiences, and to reflect on the diversity of Australian society. Migration stories do not end with arrival on Australian shores. The exhibition follows the narrative as migrants established themselves in their new country and, together with their descendants, created cultural and religious communities. Represented too are experiences of navigating and resisting racism and bureaucratic oppression, and the parallel 236-year-long First Nations resistance to colonisation of their lands, occupied and nurtured for tens of thousands of years prior to European arrival.

The National Library of Australia will continue to build collections about the lives, experiences, publications and organisations important to migrant communities. These stories enrich the national collection, just as migration has enriched Australian society, immeasurably.

Dr Marie-Louise Ayres FAHA
Director-General, National Library of Australia

HOPES AND FEARS:
Australian Migration Stories

In most homes in Australia, you will find a bookcase, a mantelpiece or a shelf with a display of family photographs. These small intimate galleries chronicle the individuals, both young and old, who populate the family tree. Sometimes the images reach back two or three generations, depicting siblings, parents and grandparents.

One of them may be of a relative who embarked on a long and difficult journey to Australia. This treasured portrait testifies to how that journey helped make possible the life the family has today. When you look at the picture of an ancestor, someone who may have spoken a different language, eaten different food and worn different clothes, it invites you to wonder why they decided to leave their home, and what it was like for them to arrive in a strange new country. What were the hopes and fears that motivated them to recast their lives in such a dramatic way?

Stories of migration are very much part of our national experience. The most recent Australian Census, conducted in 2021, tells us that more than half of Australians have at least one parent born overseas or were themselves born overseas. Coming from all parts of the globe, these migrants help make Australia one of the most diverse nations in the world. Today it is a favourite pastime for Australians to compare their backgrounds and celebrate their connection to a country or continent far away.

Exploring the history of migration to Australia starts with an important fact. First Australians have lived on this continent for at least 65,000 years. They did not cede the land that the British claimed, and they continue to assert their sovereignty. When Governor Arthur Phillip arrived on Gadigal Country with the First Fleet of 11 ships on 26 January 1788, he did not have the permission of the Gadigal people, or any other peoples of the Eora Nation, to build a settlement at Sydney Cove. The process of colonisation, which has unfolded ever since, resulted in the dispossession of the Traditional Owners from their land. First Australians resisted the British, but in most instances they were pushed off their Country. Disease, violence and coercion, and competition for resources wrought terrible damage, but Indigenous nations survived to reclaim lands and waterways, and today their cultures and languages are often resurgent.

The British occupation of Australia was part of a larger pattern of European colonisation across the globe in the seventeenth and eighteenth centuries. The European powers were searching for new territory to exploit, and the reports of explorers, especially James Cook following his expedition along the east coast of Australia in 1770, indicated that this was a land that might be successfully occupied. The first convicts, sailors and soldiers who came to Australia had little choice in the matter. After the rebellion of British colonies in north America, the imperial government sought to address the problem of overflowing prisons at home, and to stake a strategic claim in the Pacific region, by establishing a colony at Botany Bay. When Phillip arrived with the First Fleet in January 1788, he preferred Port Jackson—soon to become known as Sydney—as a more suitable site. As the colony grew, and profits from trade within the British Empire accrued, more people came.

The convicts, and the guards and officials who accompanied them, were predominantly British, but there were exceptions, such as William Blue, an African-American originally from New York. Blue was transported to Sydney in 1801 for stealing raw sugar. After finishing his sentence, he worked as a waterman, and in 1811 Governor Lachlan Macquarie appointed him harbour watchman and constable. Blue eventually became a well-known Sydney identity, nicknamed 'the Old Commodore'. His journey from convict to valued member of the community was a story that was not uncommon in early Sydney. Many convicts eventually made the transition from prisoner of the Crown to landowning settler or entrepreneur.

As such, the Australian colonies became a place where there was potential for a new start. As the colonies prospered, the convicts were followed by free settlers who came in search of cheap land and new economic opportunities. Charitable organisations sent young women from workhouses and children from orphanages. The unemployed could apply for assisted passages in the hope that the colonies would provide them with a better future.

Wealthy British investors, with ready access to capital and political influence, were able to take advantage of the opportunities on offer. Products such as whale oil, seal skins and wool offered the promise of rich returns. In 1840 the end of convict transportation to eastern mainland Australia posed a challenge, as cheap labour was required to exploit the land which had become available. To fill this gap, indentured labour was imported from India and China. Pacific islanders were brought in—sometimes without their consent—to work on plantations in the tropical north, mainly growing sugar. South Asians

(referred to as 'Afghans'), with their expertise as cameleers, migrated to assist in opening up the centre of the continent to more Europeans, thereby further contributing to the dispossession of the First Australians.

The goldrushes of the 1850s led to a population explosion as people migrated to south-eastern Australia from all over the globe, lured by the prospect of wealth. This set the scene for further unrest, based on class, race and access to land, just when the colonies were beginning to govern themselves. Unrest erupted on the Ballarat goldfields in what famously became known as the Eureka Stockade uprising of 3 December 1854. Anti-Chinese violence occurred on the goldfields in New South Wales and Victoria. Colonial governments imposed various anti-Chinese laws, including the immigration poll tax introduced in Victoria (1855), South Australia (1857) and New South Wales (1861). Chinese miners protested the laws and, by 1867, they had all been repealed. However, there was a revival of anti-Chinese sentiment and legislation in 1878, in response to Chinese migration to the Palmer River goldfields in northern Queensland, the presence of Chinese labour on merchant shipping and campaigning by politicians and union leaders. The motivation for anti-Chinese agitation was both racial, with widespread fear and prejudice against 'coloured' people, and economic, with miners and unions wanting to protect jobs and working conditions.

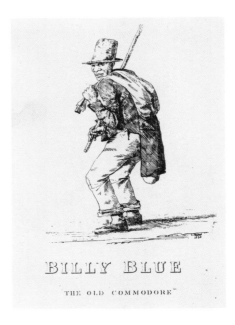

CHARLES RODIUS (1802–1860)
Billy Blue, the Old Commodore, 1834

With the coming of Federation in 1901, this desire for a British Australia was expressed in the 'White Australia policy', which was implemented through legislation such as the *Immigration Restriction Act 1901*. The Act created the machinery for a dictation test designed solely to prevent non-Europeans from entering Australia. Between 1901 and 1958, migrants could be asked to write 50 words in any European language, as dictated by an immigration officer. After 1905, the officer could choose any language. This made it easy to fail an applicant if they were from an 'undesirable' country, had a criminal record, medical issues or were thought to be 'morally unfit'.

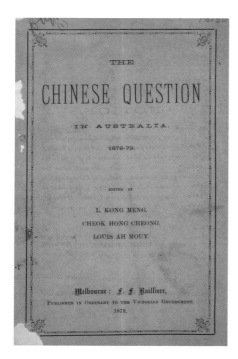

LOWE KONG MENG (co-editor, 1831–1888); CHEOK HONG CHEONG (co-editor, 1853–1928); LOUIS AH MOUY (co-editor, 1826–1918), *The Chinese Question in Australia*, 1879

The new federal parliament passed legislation that enforced the repatriation of Pacific islanders who had been brought to work on sugar plantations. The new Australian Constitution's race powers excluded the making of laws for First Australians, responsibility for whom remained exclusively with the six states until the Northern Territory passed from South Australia to the Commonwealth in 1911.

The First World War temporarily halted the flow of migrants to Australia, but it soon regathered pace in the 1920s. Britain was again targeted for workers, particularly farmers, labourers and domestic servants. More than 300,000 migrants came during the decade, many of them taking advantage of the assisted passages scheme jointly funded by the British and Australian governments. William Hughes, who was prime minister from 1915 until 1923, emphasised Australia's need to increase its British population to preserve its security; as health and repatriation minister in the 1930s, he popularised the slogan 'populate or perish'. In the lead-up to the outbreak of the Second World War the Australian Government initially resisted taking Jewish refugees, but eventually relented. More than 5,000 Jewish refugees arrived in 1939.

During the Second World War the Australian Government began planning for an expanded immigration program and, in 1945, established the Department of Immigration with Arthur Calwell as its first minister. Calwell travelled to Europe in 1947 and met with the International Refugee Organization. Australia agreed to assist with the resettlement of the millions of people displaced after the war. By 1954 more than 170,000 displaced people, mainly from the Baltic states, Poland and Eastern Europe, had arrived. New migrants helped fill factories and mines, and worked on infrastructure projects such as the Snowy Mountains Hydro-electric Scheme.

While the migration intake had been expanded to take people from across Europe there was still a strong focus on attracting British migrants to Australia. In 1945 the Assisted Passage Migration Scheme, popularly known as the 'Ten Pound Pom' scheme, allowed British migrants to come to Australia for £10 provided they were under 45 and in good health. The scheme remained in place until 1959.

From the 1950s Australian governments began to slowly dismantle the legislative framework that underpinned the White Australia policy. *The Immigration Restriction Act 1901* was superseded by the *Migration Act 1958*, under which the infamous dictation test was replaced with a system of visas. In 1966 a review of Australia's migration policy recommended that the assessment of potential migrants focus on their qualifications and suitability to settle, rather than on their race or nationality. As a result, the government began to accept a small number of migrants from Asia. In 1973 further changes were made, allowing migrants to apply for citizenship after three years of residence, regardless of race. Then Immigration Minister Al Grassby articulated a new vision of a multicultural Australia in which migrants from diverse cultural backgrounds would be celebrated for their contribution to Australian society. The migrant intake to Australia was becoming more diverse, but there was little Asian immigration until later in the 1970s.

The acceptance of refugees has been part of Australia's migration program since the 1950s. Migrants came from Hungary, after the Soviet repression of the Hungarian Revolution in 1956, and from Czechoslovakia, after the suppression of the 'Prague Spring' of 1968. They also came from Southeast Asia after the end of the Vietnam War in 1975. Political troubles and environmental factors like drought causing famines, in South America, Ethiopia and the Middle East, also prompted refugees to seek protection in Australia.

Many Chinese students successfully applied to remain in Australia in the wake of the infamous 'Tiananmen Square massacre'. Conflict in the former state of Yugoslavia in the 1990s also led to more refugees being resettled. Australia's humanitarian program continues, with refugees arriving from Iraq, Syria, Iran, Myanmar, Afghanistan, Democratic Republic of Congo, Burundi, Somalia and Sudan. Today Australia is one of the main countries committed to resettling refugees.

During the 1980s concerns about the level of unemployment led to a reduction in Australia's migration intake and a shift of focus away from assisted migration towards schemes specifically designed to attract skilled migrants to fill labour and skill shortages. Reuniting families, however, continued to be an important component of Australia's migration intake.

In the 1980s and 1990s migration became a hot political topic in Australia. Community anxiety about the impact of migration—specifically, non-European migration—on social harmony, employment and housing was reflected in increased anti-migrant rhetoric. The celebration of multicultural Australia, which had marked the 1970s, endured alongside debates about Asian and Muslim immigration and border control. In 2015 the Department of Immigration and Border Protection and the Australian Customs and Border Protection Service were amalgamated. Migrants arriving in Australia today are met by officers of the Australia Border Force, a law enforcement agency.

The history of migration to Australia has been marked by fierce debates about who should come to this country, and who should be allowed to stay. It also comprises many individual stories of those who made the journey to Australia and of their struggle to start a new life. To understand this history, we need to interrogate the evidence that has survived from the past. The *Hopes and Fears* exhibition showcases a fascinating selection of these many and varied records from Australia's migration history, all of which are available at the National Library of Australia.

GEOFF PRYOR (b. 1944), *Meanwhile, out there in battler-land ... her ghost may be heard*, 25 November 1999

THE COLONIES

The arrival of the First Fleet on Gadigal Country at Sydney Cove in 1788 brought around 1,400 convicts, sailors, soldiers and administrators to Australia. Over the next 100 years the British occupied more land, establishing settlements and dispossessing Traditional Owners.

What started as a series of precarious British outposts eventually grew to become six self-governing colonies, which claimed the entire continent and Tasmania. These colonies competed for migrants from across the British Empire.

Migrants also came from Europe, the United States, China, South Asia and the Pacific. By the 1880s Australia's population exceeded 2.25 million people. Over the same period, it is estimated that the Indigenous population fell from approximately 750,000 to less than 200,000.

Secondary punishment uniform, Van Diemen's Land, 1830s

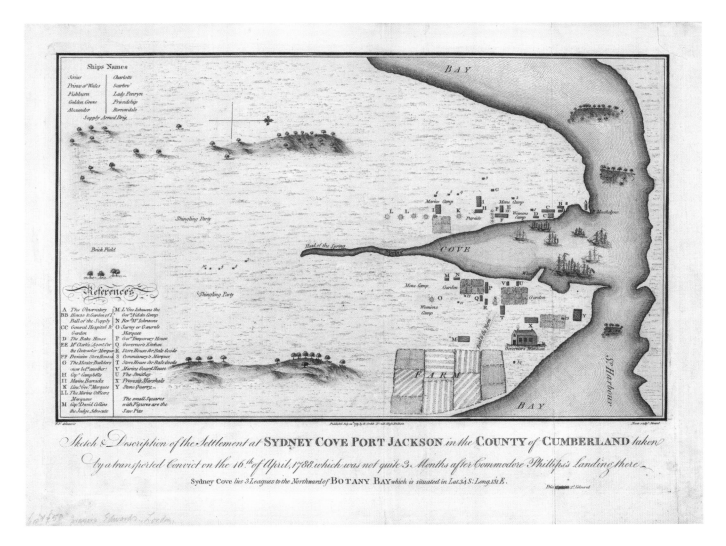

Sketch & Description of the Settlement at SYDNEY COVE PORT JACKSON in the COUNTY of CUMBERLAND taken by a transported Convict on the 16th of April, 1788. which was not quite 3 Months after Commodore Phillips's Landing there.

Sydney Cove lies 3 Leagues to the Northward of BOTANY BAY which is situated in Lat. 34 S: Long. 151 E.

PORT JACKSON, GADIGAL, CAMMERAYGAL AND WANGAL COUNTRY

This sketch, attributed to Francis Fowkes, a former navy midshipman transported for seven years for theft, was the first published map of the settlement at Port Jackson. The site was inhabited by the Gadigal, Cammeraygal and Wangal peoples of the Eora Nation, who did not cede sovereignty for this settlement. The 11 ships of the First Fleet can be seen in the harbour.

FRANCIS FOWKES (active 1788–1800), *Sydney Cove, Port Jackson, in the County of Cumberland*, 1789

AMBROISE-LOUIS GARNERAY
(1783–1857), *Portsmouth Harbour
with prison hulks*, 1814

TRANSPORTATION

Transportation of convicts was a key part of the British justice system. Throughout the seventeenth and eighteenth centuries convicts were regularly sent to the American and West Indian colonies, where they were used for forced labour. The outbreak of the American War of Independence (1775–1783) meant that convicts could no longer be transported to the American colonies, so the British government investigated other options, eventually selecting New South Wales. Between 1787 and 1852 more than 150,000 convicts were transported to the east coast of Australia.

The transportation system provided a path for convicts to become settlers. Colonial governors had the power to issue tickets of leave and pardons, which allowed convicts varying degrees of freedom. Emancipated convicts could receive a land grant, purchase land and start businesses. Other convicts, who were not serving life sentences, could gain these freedoms by completing their sentence.

Overcrowding in British jails had led to former Royal Navy ships being used as floating prisons. After sentencing, some convicts were housed in these prison hulks while awaiting transportation to Australia. The hulks were moored on the Thames and in Plymouth harbour and other British ports.

Secondary punishment uniform,
Van Diemen's Land, 1830s

A SECOND OFFENCE

The nineteenth-century British justice system was punitive and harsh. Over 200 offences carried the death penalty but transportation was often used as an alternative to execution. Most of the convicts transported to the Australian penal settlements had committed property crimes, including minor theft and burglary. Political prisoners and military deserters were also transported. Convicts who committed crimes in the colonies could be flogged, placed in shackles or sent to penal settlements such as Norfolk Island and Port Arthur, Tasmania.

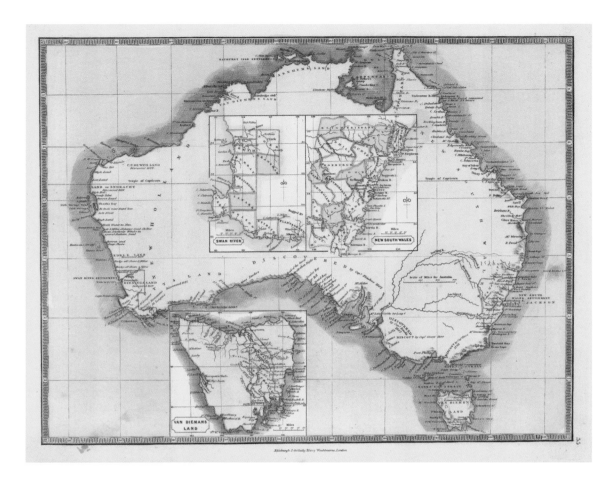

JOHN GELLATLY (1803–1856),
Map of Australia, with inset maps of the British settlements of New South Wales, Van Diemen's Land, and Swan River, 1843

THE LIMITS OF SETTLEMENT

The growing markets for wool and meat in the 1820s saw an increasing demand for land by migrants, emancipated convicts and native-born settlers. Early settlers to New South Wales could take up land in the 'Nineteen Counties'. Also known as the 'Limits of Location', these reached from Kempsey in the north to Batemans Bay in the south and Wellington in the west. In Tasmania the counties of Cornwall and Buckingham were established in 1804, and Western Australia was claimed for the British Crown in 1827.

Some pastoralists occupied land to run sheep and cattle without the approval of either the colonial government or the land's Traditional Owners. 'Squatting', as it was known, remained a feature of colonial life until the 1860s.

CAROLINE CHISHOLM.
(From a Daguerreotype by Hogg, 432, West Strand.)

THE
EMIGRANT'S GUIDE
TO
AUSTRALIA:

LONDON:
CLARKE, BEETON, & CO., FOREIGN BOOKSELLERS,
148, FLEET STREET.

1853

SOCIAL REFORMER

Caroline Chisholm was concerned that women who were brought to the colonies, without the protection of a husband, could be forced to choose between prostitution and destitution. She established a refuge for women and provided opportunities for employment in domestic service. She believed that women—or 'God's police' as she called them—could help civilise the colonies.

ENEAS MACKENZIE (active 1852–1853), *The Emigrant's Guide to Australia, with a Memoir of Mrs Chisholm*, 1853

ARTIST UNKNOWN, *Battle of Vinegar Hill*, 1804

POLITICAL PRISONERS

It is estimated that more than 3,000 political prisoners were sentenced to transportation to Australia. This included the Scottish Martyrs convicted of sedition in 1794 and rebels from the 1798 uprising in Ireland. In the nineteenth century more agitators were transported, including the Tolpuddle Martyrs in 1834, Swing Rioters in 1831 and Chartists in 1840.

This watercolour sketch depicts the clash between British forces and convict rebels at Castle Hill, New South Wales, in 1804. The convicts were led by veterans of the Society of United Irishmen who had been transported from Ireland to New South Wales following the Irish Rebellion of 1798. The convict uprising was mercilessly put down by British troops.

SOUTH SEA WHALING

Britannia, a whaling ship, was one of the 11 vessels of the Third Fleet, which departed Portsmouth, England, in 1791. The voyage took 201 days. Of the 150 convicts on board, 21 died on route. After disembarking the convicts in Sydney, *Britannia* set out on a successful whaling expedition. Credited as the first European killing of whales in the South Seas, the expedition marked the start of that industry in the colonies. It would be the major export industry until overtaken by wool in the 1830s.

THOMAS WHITCOMBE (1763–1824),
Departure of the whaler Britannia from Sydney Cove, 1798

LIONEL LINDSAY (1874–1961),
Whalers' Arms, The Rocks, Sydney,
1912

MĀORI IN SYDNEY

Māori were among the earliest
groups to establish themselves in
Sydney. They were part of a trading
network with New Zealand and
worked on many of the ships based
in Port Jackson. Lionel Lindsay
celebrated Sydney's Māori history
with this sketch of the Whalers'
Arms in Māori Lane in The Rocks
area of Sydney.

MEN OF CAPITAL

The Australian Agricultural Company (AAC) was formed by an Act of the British Parliament in 1824 that provided for a Crown grant of 1,000,000 acres in the Port Stephens area on the mid-north coast of New South Wales. The concepts of Indigenous land ownership and the perspective of the Traditional Owners, the Worimi people, were not considered. With money from British investors, and access to cheap convict labour, as well as indentured labourers from Britain, China and Germany, and Aboriginal men and women, the AAC was able to exploit the resources of the Karuah River valley and the Gloucester flats.

The AAC's first chief agent in New South Wales was Robert Dawson. Dawson published an account of the company's early years, *The Present State of Australia: a Description of the Country, Its Advantages and Prospects, with Reference to Emigration; and a Particular Account of the Manners, Customs and Condition of Its Aboriginal Inhabitants* in 1830. While giving a positive account of his own interactions with Indigenous people, Dawson also included eyewitness accounts from Indigenous people describing how cedar cutters 'had shot their relations and friends'. Dawson lamented that he had been shown 'many orphans, whose parents had fallen by the hands of white men'.

AUSTRALIAN AGRICULTURAL COMPANY (issuer), *Australian Agricultural Company share certificate*, 1825

GEORGE FRENCH ANGAS (artist, 1822–1886); JAMES W. GILES (lithographer, 1801–1870), *Klemsic [Klemzig], a village of German settlers near Adelaide*, 1847

RELIGIOUS REFUGEES

By the 1830s King Frederick William III of Prussia had imposed his version of the Protestant liturgy on his subjects. Pastors who did not conform were sent to prison. In 1838 Pastor August Kavel arranged, through George Fife Angas, Director of the South Australian Company (the artist's father), for finance to take himself and his congregation of Old Lutherans, who were opposed to the king's changes, from their village of Klemzig (now Klepsk, Poland) to South Australia. The initial 517 refugees were soon joined by more. They settled first in the Torrens Valley, where they built a village in their traditional style.

PENNYS STOPES. B.B. MINE.
APRIL 12ᵗʰ 47

EXPERT MINERS

Mining towns such as Camborne and Redruth in Cornwall struggled economically in the 1830s–1840s. Local potato crops were destroyed by blight in 1845 and 1846. However, the discovery, in the new colony of South Australia, of silver-lead at Glen Osmond by two Cornish miners in the late 1830s, and then of copper at Kapunda in 1842 and Burra in 1845, caused immense excitement. Between 1846 and 1850 there were 4,775 government emigrants who travelled from Cornwall to South Australia, representing 27 per cent of all arrivals in the colony. They mostly came to the copper mines.

SAMUEL THOMAS GILL (1818–1880), *Pennys Stopes, B.B. [Burra Burra] Mine, 12 April 1847*, 1847

GOLD AND EXPLORATION

The discovery of gold at Ophir, New South Wales, and at Clunes, Victoria, in 1851 marked the beginning of Australia's goldrushes. Migrants from all over the world brought new skills and professions, changing convict colonies into progressive cities. In response to racial conflict, colonial governments implemented the first wave of anti-Chinese legislation in Victoria (1855), South Australia (1857) and New South Wales (1861). These laws were repealed by 1867 after sustained resistance from Chinese people and their European allies.

European explorers made their way across the continent in the 1860s, opening up land for pastoral and agricultural industries. However, in doing so, they hastened Indigenous dispossession and environmental change.

EDWIN STOCQUELER (1829–1895), *Australian gold diggings*, c. 1855

CHINESE SLUICING, NEAR BEECHWORTH [FROM A SKETCH BY N. CHEVALIER, ESQ].—SEE PAGE 10.

CHANGING THE LANDSCAPE

In 1852 gold was discovered at Spring Creek, Beechworth, part of the Ovens Valley goldfield. Within a year more than 8,000 miners arrived, including people from the Sze Yap, Sam Yap and Chungshan regions in southern China. By 1868 the Beechworth area was home to one-third of the entire Chinese population of Victoria. Many were employed by sluicing companies while others worked their own small claims.

NICHOLAS CHEVALIER (artist, 1828–1902); FREDERICK GROSSE (engraver, 1828–1894), *Chinese people ground-sluicing, near Beechworth, Victoria*, 1867

YACKADUNA (AKA TOMMY MCRAE)
(c. 1835–1901), *Aboriginal man and Chinese man, and Aboriginal men fighting*, 1881

A FIRST NATIONS WITNESS

Yackaduna (Tommy McRae) was a Kwat Kwat and Wurundjeri man, and a widely known and respected artist with connections to Country in north-east Victoria, who covered the Ovens Valley goldfields. From 1838 onwards First Nations people and squatters in this area were involved in several violent confrontations in which people on both sides were killed. In 1852 gold was discovered. Racial tensions culminated in the Buckland anti-Chinese riot of 4 July 1857, when about 100 Europeans attacked the Chinese settlements. At least three Chinese people died. Yackaduna either witnessed or knew of these events. By the 1880s he was at Wahgunyah, selling his drawings of traditional Aboriginal life, squatters and Chinese people to European collectors.

TRANSPORTING SUPPLIES

From the mid-1800s until the late 1920s teams of Muslim and Sikh cameleers from the arid hills and plains of Afghanistan and British India were brought to Australia. They were thought to be the most reliable method of transporting goods through the arid regions of outback Australia. The cameleers belonged to four main groups (Pashtun, Baloch, Punjabi and Sindhi), and spoke a variety of languages such as Pashto, Dari (Persian), Baluchi, Punjabi, Sindhi and Urdu.

As they learned about the Australian bush and society, they began their own businesses. By the 1890s they dominated the camel business, travelling between the Indian subcontinent and Australia to import camels and goods. While many returned home upon completing their work contracts, others stayed in Australia and established families.

JOHN FLYNN (1880–1951),
An 'Afghan' camel driver with two unknown men, standing next to a camel train, c. 1912–1930

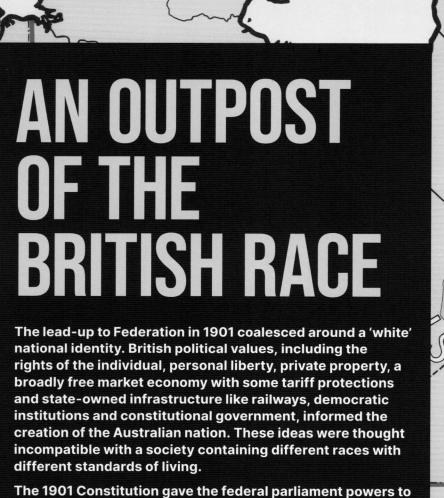

AN OUTPOST OF THE BRITISH RACE

The lead-up to Federation in 1901 coalesced around a 'white' national identity. British political values, including the rights of the individual, personal liberty, private property, a broadly free market economy with some tariff protections and state-owned infrastructure like railways, democratic institutions and constitutional government, informed the creation of the Australian nation. These ideas were thought incompatible with a society containing different races with different standards of living.

The 1901 Constitution gave the federal parliament powers to make laws regarding 'people of any race'—except Aboriginal people—and issues such as 'immigration and emigration', 'naturalisation and aliens' and the 'influx of criminals', all of which underpinned the laws that would make up the White Australia policy.

THOMAS GRIFFITH TAYLOR (1880–1963),
The New Oxford Wall Maps of Australia,
c. 1920

Recruits ~ Boats crew ~ New Hebrides ~ Queensland Labor Traffic

A.LOMER & C?. PHOTOGRAPHERS.

'BLACKBIRDING'

The practice of recruiting labourers from South Sea islands was popularly known as 'blackbirding'. While many South Sea Islanders agreed to work as indentured labourers, there were also many examples of workers being kidnapped or tricked into coming to Australia.

Between 1863 and 1904 an estimated 55,000 to 62,500 South Sea Islanders were brought to Australia to labour on sugarcane, cotton and pineapple plantations in Queensland and northern New South Wales. The use of islander labour reflected a widespread belief that 'whites' were not well adapted for work in the tropics. Indentured labour was also attractive because of its comparatively lower cost.

In 1901 the new Australian federal parliament passed the *Pacific Island Labourers Act*, which enacted a law to deport the majority of Pacific Islanders living in Australia. Only 700 out of about 10,000 were exempt from deportation.

ALBERT LOMER AND CO., *Recruiters and boat's crew, New Hebrides, Queensland labour traffic*, c. 1890

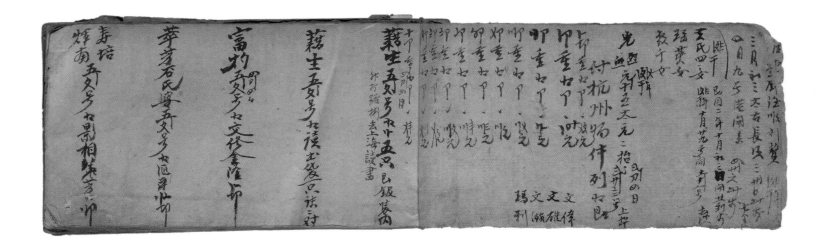

KWONG SUE DUK (1853–1929),
Account book, c. 1913–1920s

THE CANTONESE PACIFIC

Gold rush migrants from the Cantonese-speaking counties of southern China created loosely integrated communities around the Pacific rim in English-speaking settler societies, using colonial Hong Kong as a hub from which to continue family and business links. The scale of movement between these communities drove the development of cross-Pacific shipping routes in the late nineteenth and early twentieth centuries.

Kwong Sue Duk travelled to the Californian goldfields, then returned home to Toisan, China. In 1875 he migrated to Cooktown, Queensland, but later went home again to study traditional Chinese medicine. In 1882 he moved to Southport, Northern Territory, where he established the Sun Mow Loong general store. Naturalised in 1884, he moved to Darwin where he built a general store known as the Stonehouses. He had extensive business interests in Queensland, the Northern Territory and Victoria, while his four wives and 24 children were spread across China, Australia and the United States.

ABOVE: MAKER UNKNOWN, *Christening gown first worn by Kwong Mui Ying (May), and later by other members of Kwong Sue Duk's family*, 1901

LEFT: PHOTOGRAPHER UNKNOWN, *Kwong Mui Ying (May), first daughter of Kwong Sue Duk's fourth wife, Wong Kwei Far*, 1918

KEEPING FAMILY TIES

Kwong Mui Ying (May) was born in Darwin, so she was exempt from the dictation test administered under the *Immigration Restriction Act 1901*, which was designed to limit non-white immigration. In 1918 May Kwong married Charles Way Lee, a cabinet-maker, in Geelong, Victoria. Way Lee was born in Canton, China, in 1884 and arrived in Cooktown, Queensland, in 1901. He demonstrated good character in order to apply for a Certificate of Exemption from the dictation test, which allowed non-British subjects resident in Australia to return after travelling overseas. Despite Australia's immigration restrictions, the family was able to travel for personal or business reasons, but May and her Melbourne-born children, Stella Love and Shing Joe, had to produce their birth certificates whenever they left for China or returned to Australia.

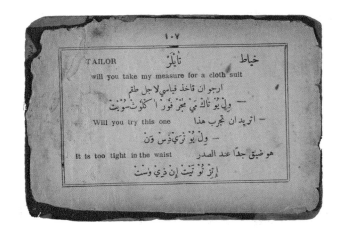

ABOVE LEFT: PHOTOGRAPHER UNKNOWN, *Anthony Wehby, Braidwood, Victoria*, c. 1912

ABOVE RIGHT: *English-to-Arabic Dictionary carried by Anthony George Wehby*, 1910

RIGHT: *Invoice and order form from Stanton Melick, Warehousemen & Manufacturers, Redfern, to Mr A.G. Wehby, Braidwood*, 12 May 1931

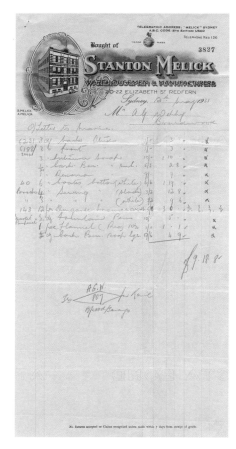

FAMILY AND BUSINESS

By the 1890s Lebanese people—or 'Syrians', as they were classified by colonial authorities—were migrating to Australia in small but increasing numbers. Some were well-educated and wealthy, looking for economic opportunities. They brought out family and fellow villagers to help build their networks and businesses. The *Naturalisation Act 1903* barred new arrivals from being naturalised as they were classed as Asian.

Constantine Nicholas (Stanton) Melick was born in the village of Bterram and migrated to Sydney in 1888. He worked as a hawker of cloth and fancy goods before going on to establish a cloth warehousing and manufacturing business in Redfern.

Anthony George Wehby migrated to Australia with his father in 1891, settling in Rockhampton, Queensland. Wehby married Constantine Melick's niece, Faredah. Then, in 1912, the family moved to Braidwood, New South Wales, where Anthony and Faredah set up a general store and drapery business.

Marie Bashir's school report card for grade 3, c. 1930

BRAIDWOOD PUBLIC SCHOOL.
"PLAY THE GAME"
Report Form.

This Report is furnished in the interests of each individual child to secure co-operation of the parents when indifferent reports are furnished.

Name _Marie Bashir_   Class _3rd_

Subject	Possible Marks	Marks Gained	Position in Class	REMARKS
READING	100	88	1	Very good
WRITING	100	66	3	must be neater
ARITHMETIC	100	92	1	Very good
COMPOSITION Grammar	100	92	1	Good work.
SPELLING	100	95	1	Excellent
POETRY	100	80	1	Very good
History	100	86	1	Very good
Geography	100	89	1	most pleasing work.
TOTAL	800	688		

Number in Class _11_   Position in Class _1st_

HOMEWORK _Satisfactory_

CONDUCT _A very noisy worker._

ATTENDANCE _Satisfactory_

PROGRESS _Most satisfactory_

PRINCIPAL'S REPORT

Marie has been doing splendid work since she came to this school. Her general knowledge is good but she is far too talkative.

FOR Parent's Signature _M. Wehby._   Teacher's Signature _J Willshire_

J. R. McQUALTER, Headmaster.

A DISTINGUISHED DESCENDANT

Marie Bashir was born in 1930, to Michael Bashir, who established a manchester and menswear business in the Riverina town of Narrandera, and his wife, Victoria, daughter of Abraham Melick (Constantine Melick's younger brother). The couple had met while Victoria was employed as a secretary in the Melick family business. Michael had interrupted his medical studies at the American University of Beirut to visit Australia.

Bashir attended Braidwood Public School, staying with May Wehby, her maternal cousin. She completed her medical degree at the University of Sydney in 1956 and embarked on a distinguished career in medicine and psychiatry. On 1 March 2001 Bashir became the first woman to be appointed governor of New South Wales.

JOHN FLYNN (1880–1951),
*Japanese pearl divers, Broome,
Western Australia*, c. 1914

'NOT SUITABLE FOR WHITE MEN'

During the 1880s and 1890s
Japanese indentured labourers
began working in pearling industries
in northern Queensland and the
north-west coast of Australia,
alongside Filipinos and Malays.
The *Immigration Restriction Act
1901* contained an exemption for
the 'master and crew of any public
vessel' enabling the pearling industry
to be Australia's sole exemption to
the policy of excluding indentured
coloured labour. This was to keep
costs low, and because there was a
belief that pearl shell diving was too
dangerous for white men—almost
3 per cent of all divers employed
between 1898 and 1903 died plying
their trade.

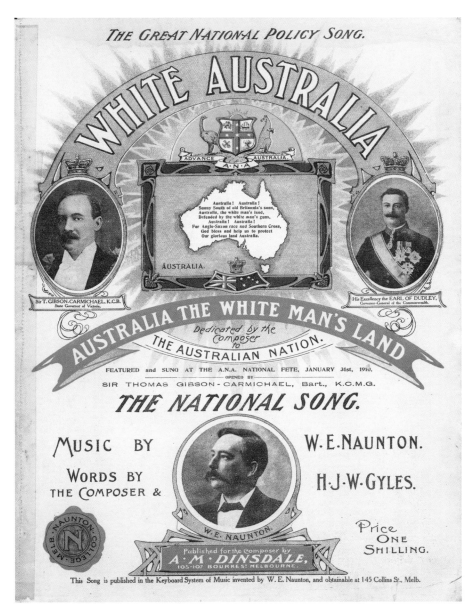

WILLIAM EMANUEL NAUNTON
(words and music, 1871–1939);
HARRY JOHN WILLMOTT GYLES
(words, 1880–1959), *White Australia:
The Great National Policy Song*, 1910

'THE NATIONAL SONG'

This song was a choral celebration of the White Australia policy. The words articulate a vision of an Australia settled by Britain's surplus population in which 'coloured' immigration would not be allowed. The chorus makes it clear how British sovereignty would be enforced: 'Australia, the white man's land, Defended by the white man's guns'.

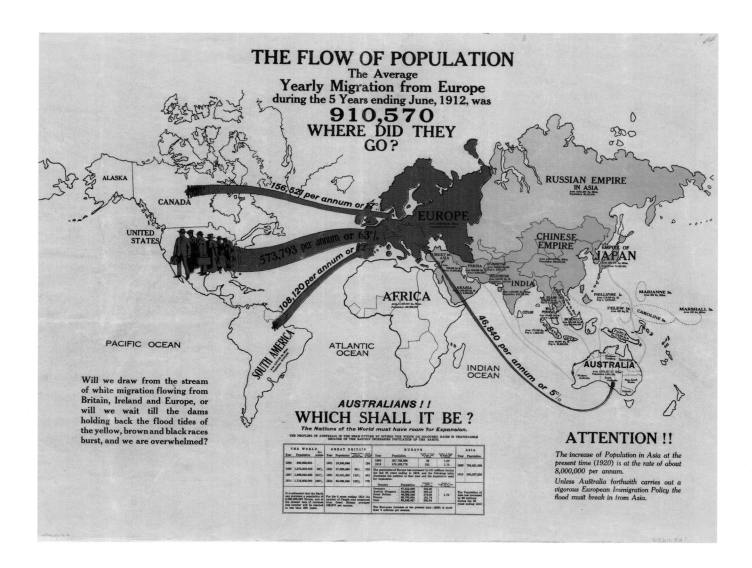

MAKER UNKNOWN, *The Flow of Population*, 1920

'POPULATE OR PERISH'

After the First World War political leaders and journalists argued that Australia needed to increase the rate of British migration without delay. This was motivated by a fear of being overwhelmed by the rapidly growing population of Asia. In the 1920s more than 200,000 British migrants came to Australia under a range of assisted migration schemes.

PHOTOGRAPHER UNKNOWN, *A Chinese-Australian in his market garden, Northern Territory*, c. 1930

FEEDING THE POPULATION

From the 1880s to 1930s Chinese market gardeners were essential to the survival of many Australian towns. In 1878 the editor of the *South Australian Register* noted that without Chinese farmers there would be scarcely any vegetables to feed the residents of the Northern Territory. They grew a range of tropical crops, many of which were familiar to them from southern China. These included sweet potatoes, peanuts and bananas, as well as temperate crops more familiar to Europeans, such as cabbages and cucumbers.

PHOTOGRAPHER UNKNOWN,
Seamen's Union General Secretary Tom Walsh (centre, with his wife, Adela Pankhurst Walsh, at his left) and Assistant Secretary Jacob Johnson on their way to their deportation hearing at Darlinghurst Courthouse, Sydney, 3 September 1925

POLITICAL TARGETS

In 1925 new categories targeting political activists were added to the *Immigration Restriction Act 1901*. Tom Walsh and Jacob 'Jack' Johnson were officials of the Federated Seamen's Union of Australasia. The government deregistered the union, and Walsh and Johnson were charged with inciting the Waterside Workers' Federation of Australia to strike. When the union supported a British seamen's strike against a 10 per cent wage cut in August, Walsh and Johnson were held at Sydney's Garden Island, pending an appeal against their deportation order, which was upheld.

Walsh had migrated from Ireland in 1893. His wife, Adela Pankhurst Walsh, a British-born suffragette, had been threatened with deportation in 1917 after she spearheaded a protest against rising food prices. Johnson had migrated from the Netherlands in 1910 and was naturalised in 1913.

TOP: THEODOR ENGEL (1886–1978), *Study of Professor Mayer, a Dunera Boy, at Tatura, Victoria*, 1942

BOTTOM: THEODOR ENGEL (1886–1978), *Watercolour of Hay Internment Camp*, 1941

THE DUNERA BOYS

Theodor Engel, an engineer from Austria, was one of the 'Dunera Boys', a group of more than 2,500 men and boys (the majority of whom were Jewish) deported from Britain to Australia aboard HMT *Dunera* in mid-1940. Many of the men were musicians, artists, philosophers, scientists or writers who had sought refuge from Nazi persecution. When war broke out in 1939, they were classed as 'enemy aliens' and interned. The Dunera Boys were eventually sent to internment camps at Orange and Hay in New South Wales and Tatura in Victoria. Engel used different art styles to depict life in the Hay and Tatura camps.

THE LAND OF OPPORTUNITY

IRRIGATION ENTERPRISES

SELLING A DREAM

After Federation in 1901 competition for British migrants was fierce. In addition to the Commonwealth's promotion of migration programs, state governments also ran their own advertising campaigns, promoting the virtues of moving to particular regions in Australia. Shipping companies such as the Commonwealth Line and P&O advertised cruises to Australia. The imagery used in the advertising material focussed on the economic opportunities and healthy lifestyle available for migrants. Australia was often depicted as an agricultural paradise populated by robust 'white' farmers.

The First World War temporarily halted the flow of migrants to Australia, but it soon regathered pace in the 1920s. Britain was again targeted as a potential source of workers, particularly farmers, labourers and domestic servants.

JAMES NORTHFIELD (illustrator, 1887–1973); COMMONWEALTH IMMIGRATION OFFICE (issuer), *The Land of Opportunity: Australia's Irrigation Enterprises*, 1924

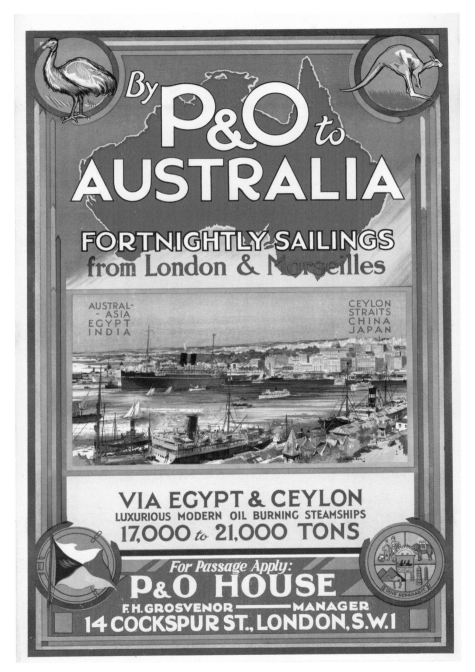

CHARLES DIXON (1872–1934), *By P&O to Australia: Fortnightly Sailings from London and Marseilles: Australasia, Egypt, India, Ceylon, Straits, China, Japan, via Egypt and Ceylon*, 1928

P&O

The Peninsular and Oriental Steam Navigation Company (P&O) was one of the major shipping lines on the Britain-to-Australia route. P&O's first voyages began in the 1850s, but it was after the Second World War that the company brought more than 1 million British migrants to Australia. The poster features the 21,000-ton liner RMS *Mooltan*. Launched in 1923, it was one of the largest ships that could pass through the Suez Canal.

THE INTELLIGENCE AND TOURIST
BUREAU, *South Australia for the Fruit
Grower*, c. 1919

NEW PASTURES

This booklet outlines the
opportunities in South Australia's
fruit-growing industry to intending
migrants. British subjects were
permitted to nominate family
members who met the criteria or
agricultural workers for assisted
passage to South Australia.

COMMONWEALTH IMMIGRATION OFFICE, *Tropical Agriculture in Australia*, c. 1921

AGRICULTURE UP NORTH

This booklet outlined opportunities for European agricultural workers in Queensland's sugarcane and dairy industries. Intending settlers were offered advances for the purchase of freehold properties, licences and leases from the Crown, to be repaid after five years.

MINISTER OF EXTERNAL AFFAIRS,
Australia: The Land of Sunshine Health & Prosperity, c. 1915

AN INVITATION

The reverse of this calendar invited migrants to 'Come to Australia', and described the sort of life and conditions they could expect to find.

SERVANTS OF EMPIRE

Between the world wars, domestic service continued to be regarded as one of the pillars of British civilisation with the British government adopting an aggressive approach to female emigration to countries such as Australia, Canada, the United States, South Africa and New Zealand. Between 1926 and 1930 the Australian and British governments jointly funded a specialised centre in Market Harborough, Leicestershire, to train women for domestic service prior to migration to Australia.

LEFT: COMMONWEALTH IMMIGRATION OFFICE (1920–1927), *Australia's Offer to the British Boy*, 1922

RIGHT: COMMONWEALTH IMMIGRATION OFFICE (1920–1927), *Australia Invites the British Domestic Girl*, 1924

PHOTOGRAPHER UNKNOWN,
Protest against treatment of British soldier-settlers outside Australia House, London, 1938

LAND FIT FOR HEROES?

The First World War created massive social and economic disruption across Europe. In Britain the 1919 Overseas Settlement Committee provided assisted passage to other parts of the empire for ex-servicemen and their families. It was followed by the *Empire Settlement Act 1922*, which promoted partnerships between Britain and various national and provincial governments throughout the empire, to help resettle British families on 'unexploited rural lands'.

However, many of these schemes, like those for returned Australian soldiers, failed. The blocks of land allocated to British and Australian soldier-settlers were too small to be viable. They required skills, such as removing trees, that the settlers did not have, and they were located too far from reliable water, transport and infrastructure. Many soldiers also returned to Australia with physical and psychological scars from their wartime experiences.

EVER OPEN DOOR

In 1866 Thomas John Barnardo founded a charity in London's East End to care for and educate children left orphaned and destitute by a recent cholera outbreak. Four years later he founded a boys' orphanage, and later a girls' home. By the time he died in 1905, his charity was caring for more than 8,500 children in 96 locations. However, he was accused of kidnapping children—a charge he admitted to, describing his actions as 'philanthrophic abduction'.

Sending children overseas helped to populate the empire, and enabled Barnardo's Homes to operate its 'ever open door' policy for British destitute children. Over a century, until the 1960s, Barnardo's Homes sent 2,784 children out to Australia from Britain. The experience of children brought to Australia by charities was investigated by the Senate, with a formal apology to the 'Forgotten Australians and former child migrants' made by Prime Minister Kevin Rudd in 2009.

JOHN MULLIGAN (1927–1996), *Teenage and child immigrants from Great Britain brought out by Dr Barnardo's on the P&O liner Canberra*, 10 October 1963

BECOMING AUSTRALIAN

During the later years of the Second World War, the Australian Government began planning for an expanded immigration program. A rapidly growing population was seen as the best way to defend a nation that had feared a Japanese invasion during the war. A target of 70,000 migrants a year was set, and while the emphasis was on British migrants, the government began an advertising campaign to encourage the Australian public to accept a wider range of European migrants.

All self-governing nations of the Commonwealth agreed that each nation could define its own citizenship in 1947. The *Australian Nationality and Citizenship Act 1948* was used as an incentive to encourage non-British migrants to assimilate so they could be rewarded with full citizenship. The White Australia policy began to be dismantled, starting in 1958 when the infamous dictation test was replaced by a visa system. From 1966 potential migrants were assessed by their qualifications and suitability to settle rather than by their race or nationality. In 1973 further changes were made, and migrants became eligible to apply for citizenship after three years of residence, regardless of race.

In the 1970s Australia moved beyond assimilationist policies to a new vision of a multicultural Australia. The country's migrant intake was becoming more diverse than it had ever been.

PHOTOGRAPHER UNKNOWN, *Verners and Girts Linde with their mural for the arts and craft exhibition at the Australian Citizenship Convention*, 1950

ARTIST UNKNOWN, *Program presented to the Honourable Arthur Calwell, Minister for Immigration*, 1949

WELCOME TO BONEGILLA

In 1947 the military camp at Bonegilla, in north-east Victoria, was acquired as a reception centre for migrants, mostly from Europe. Between then and its closure in 1971, the reception centre acted as a temporary home for more than 320,000 migrants. At the centre, migrants were taught English and learned about life in Australia, before being sent to work in areas where there were labour shortages. In 1952, and again in 1961, Bonegilla residents rioted over long waits for promised work. Immigration Minister Arthur Calwell made numerous visits to the camp during his term in office.

ARTHUR CALWELL (1896–1973), *20,000,000 Australians in Our Time! Statement of Immigration Policy by the Minister for Immigration, the Hon. Arthur A. Calwell, to the House of Representatives*, 8 September 1949

SECURING AUSTRALIA

> *There can be no argument against immigration at this period of Australian history. We must fill this country or we will lose it. But even if there were no urgent security reason for our immigration drive, there would be sound and cogent economic ones.*

Arthur Calwell was the inaugural Minister for Immigration in the Chifley Labor government (1945–1949), and the chief architect of Australia's postwar immigration drive. He planned a population growth target of 2 per cent per annum, of which half would be derived from net immigration. While he welcomed continental Europeans alongside the British in his migration programs, he was a staunch advocate of the White Australia policy and deported Malayan, Indo-Chinese and Chinese wartime refugees despite some of them having married Australian citizens and started families here.

20,000,000 AUSTRALIANS IN OUR TIME!

Statement of Immigration Policy by the Minister for Immigration, the Hon. Arthur A. Calwell, M.H.R., to the House of Representatives, September 8, 1949

PHOTOGRAPHER UNKNOWN, *The Gamboa family reunited in Australia*, 1952

A FAMILY SPLIT BY RACE

Why did they let me marry an Australian girl if they wouldn't let me into the country to see her?

Lorenzo Abrogar Gamboa was born in Pangasinan, Philippines, in 1918. He joined the US army and in 1942 was stationed in Melbourne, where he met and married Joyce Cain. In 1946 the Department of Immigration gave him three months to leave the country. Leaving behind his pregnant wife and their son, Gamboa travelled to the United States, where he took up citizenship on the basis of his military service and rejoined the army.

The Australian Government refused Gamboa entry to Australia, citing his race as the reason. A journalist reported on the family's situation, causing international embarrassment for Australia. Gamboa was finally able to reunite with Joyce and their children, Raymond and Julie, in 1951.

PHOTOGRAPHER UNKNOWN,
*Verners and Girts Linde with their
mural for the arts and craft exhibition
at the Australian Citizenship
Convention*, 1950

PAINTING LABOUR

Verners Linde and his son, Girts, fled Latvia during the Second World War.
They arrived in Fremantle in 1949, and Girts worked as a labourer, waiter
and cook throughout Western Australia, despite repeated assertions by
both father and son to immigration officials that they were artists. When
the Department of Immigration sought submissions for an exhibition of 'new
Australian' art to accompany the first Australian Citizenship Convention in
1950, the Lindes submitted a small visual proposal, which was accepted. The
resulting mural-sized painting depicted an enthusiastic group of European
migrant labourers as cultivators and builders of the nation. The mural is now
on display at Telopea Park School, Canberra.

THE NEW AUSTRALIANS' CULTURAL ASSOCIATION, *Testimonials presented to the people of Australia and the government by European migrants to Australia, on the occasion of the Australian Citizenship Convention, Canberra*, 1953

ART AND ASSIMILATION

The New Australians' Cultural Association was formed in Sydney in 1949. It aimed to welcome newcomers to Australia and introduce them to Australian art and literature, and also to advance Australian cultural development through the knowledge and experience of New Australians. The testimonials in this book were created by organisations and individuals representing Bulgarians, Croatians, Czechoslovakians, Estonians, Greeks, Hungarians, Italians, Latvians, Lebanese, Lithuanians, Dutch, Poles, Serbians, Slovakians, Ukrainians and White Russians (Russians opposed to the Bolshevik communist revolution in the period 1917–1923).

From 1950 the Australian Government promoted migrant art at its Citizenship Conventions through exhibitions that emphasised 'infusion, integration and development instead of preservation'. These displays publicised 'the community outlook between the farmers, the factory workers, the professional men and the scientists among Old and New Australians' and demonstrated how migrant arts could 'enrich the life of the whole Australian community'.

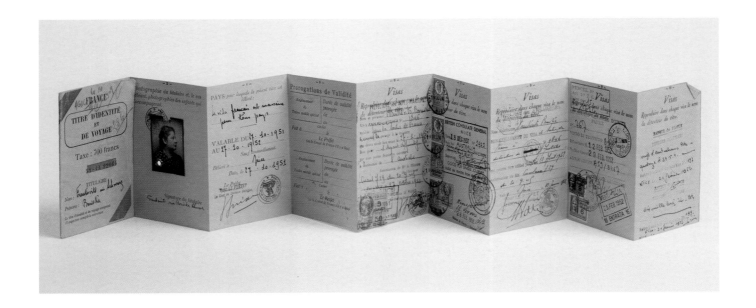

ABOVE: *Boriska Frankovits's French identity document*, 1951
RIGHT: *Yellow Star of David badge worn by Marcel Frankovits*, 1940–1944

A MARKED MAN

All Jews aged six and over were forced to wear a yellow Star of David badge, bearing the word 'Juif' (French for 'Jew'), during the Nazi occupation of France from May 1940 to December 1944. Marcel Frankovits' family survived the Holocaust, in which six million Jews were killed across Europe.

I left my country Romania the 16.8.1938 and lived here like refugee until 1944 on my saving as I had then no rights to work in France. The February 27th 1944 I was compelled by the occupation authorities to leave France for Romania following an arrangement between Romanian and German governments. The 30.6.47 I left Romania for good because of the Russian occupation. Ever since I live in Nice working together with my wife as tailors.

Meanwhile, their two sons were farmed out for their protection, Thomas to a Catholic boarding school and André to a courageous Catholic family.

TOP: *Ford employee badge belonging to Thomas Frankovits*, c. 1950

BOTTOM: *Thomas Frankovits' driver's licence*, 1948

SPONSORING THE FAMILY

Marcel and Boriska Frankovits were Romanian Jews who had fled to France during the Second World War. In 1950 the Frankovits family applied through an American Jewish migration scheme to migrate to the United States but were refused. They were advised that their eldest son, Thomas, should migrate to Australia and work in his trade as a mechanic, then sponsor his parents and younger brother, André. Thomas arrived in Sydney in 1950 and worked at Ford as a fitter, sponsoring his parents and brother in 1951. Marcel and Boriska opened a business manufacturing bags to support themselves in Sydney. André became involved with the Sydney Push, a left-wing libertarian group of bohemian artists and thinkers, and has had a career in international human rights.

ARTIST UNKNOWN, *£10 Takes You to Australia: Children under 19 Go Free!*, c. 1960

'TEN POUND POMS'

The £10 assisted passage migration scheme was established by the Commonwealth government in 1945. It provided for subsidised travel and accommodation for British migrants. Migrants were required to surrender their passports on arrival and were required to stay for at least two years. The scheme remained in place until 1981.

ARTIST UNKNOWN, *Australia: Lloyd Triestino: MN Australia, MN Oceania, MN Neptunia*, c. 1957–1963

TRIESTINO TRIO

The 'Triestino Trio'—MN *Australia*, MN *Oceania* and MN *Neptunia*—were built in the same shipyard in the 1950s and spent their entire careers operating together. Between 1957 and 1963 they transported close to 200,000 postwar migrants from Italy to Australia.

JOE GREENBERG (1923–2007)
Australia: Land of Tomorrow, c. 1948

A WORKERS' PARADISE

A central vision of the Labor government after the Second World War was to build a prosperous society without unemployment. This was outlined in a document: *Full Employment in Australia,* which was tabled in Parliament on 30 May 1945. Large-scale immigration of labour was essential to achieving this vision. The Commonwealth government embarked on an overseas advertising campaign to attract workers for agricultural and manufacturing industries alongside making immigration agreements with Britain and other nations.

There's a man's job for you IN AUSTRALIA

FILLING A SKILLS SHORTAGE

Unlike the immigration schemes of the 1920s where state governments had the responsibility of placing migrants in employment, the Commonwealth-States agreement reached on 19 August 1945 made migrant employment a Commonwealth responsibility. A target of 70,000 immigrants was proposed and it was intended to be predominantly British. However, agreements were made with other industrialised countries of northern Europe like the Netherlands, whose populations were perceived to have the skills urgently required by industry.

WOLFGANG SIEVERS (1913–2007),
*Tunnel work at T-2, Snowy
Mountains Hydro-electric Scheme*,
1957

MEN OF THE SNOWY

In 1949 work began on the Snowy Mountains Hydro-electric Scheme,
a 25-year endeavour involving the construction of 16 dams, seven power
stations, and 225 kilometres of tunnels, pipelines and aqueducts. More than
100,000 people were employed on the project, including at least 60,000
migrants from more than 30 countries, mostly from southern and eastern
Europe. The project gradually came to be seen as a demonstration of the
successful integration of migrant workers into Australian society. The scheme
is regarded by many as one of the great success stories in the development
of multiculturalism in Australia.

DIPLOMACY AND UNDERSTANDING

The Colombo Plan was an agreement between seven Commonwealth countries to form an organisation for the socio-economic development of newly independent, less developed countries. One aspect of this scheme was the provision of scholarships to Asian students. Between 1951 and 1964 Australia hosted nearly 5,500 students and trainees on Colombo Plan scholarships from South and Southeast Asia. The original intention behind the scholarships was for students to return home with positive experiences to share with their families and colleagues. However, some of these and other privately funded Asian students stayed.

The 1966 review of Australia's immigration policy noted Australia's increasingly complex involvement with Asia, including privately funded and Colombo plan students. Liberal Prime Minister Robert Menzies stated that 'the daily association of Australians with students and scholars from Asian countries has greatly widened the experience and understanding of our own people'.

CENTRAL OFFICE OF INFORMATION, GREAT BRITAIN, *The Colombo Plan*, 1969

ERN MCQUILLAN (1926–2018),
*Turkish migrants in the dining hall of
the Villawood Migrant Hostel*, 1968

A TURKISH FAMILY AT VILLAWOOD

Refugees and assisted migrants in postwar Australia were offered housing in government hostels, such as the Villawood Migrant Hostel in Sydney. Many Villawood residents later found employment in Canterbury-Bankstown, and contributed to the growth of Western Sydney. In 1976 the hostel became the Villawood Immigration Detention Centre.

Large-scale Turkish migration to Australia began after the Australia–Turkey Migration Agreement was signed in October 1967. As Australia's first migration agreement signed with a non-European nation, this was a significant milestone in the gradual dismantling of the White Australia policy. Between 1966 and 1971 the Turkish-born community in Australia grew from 2,500 to 11,589.

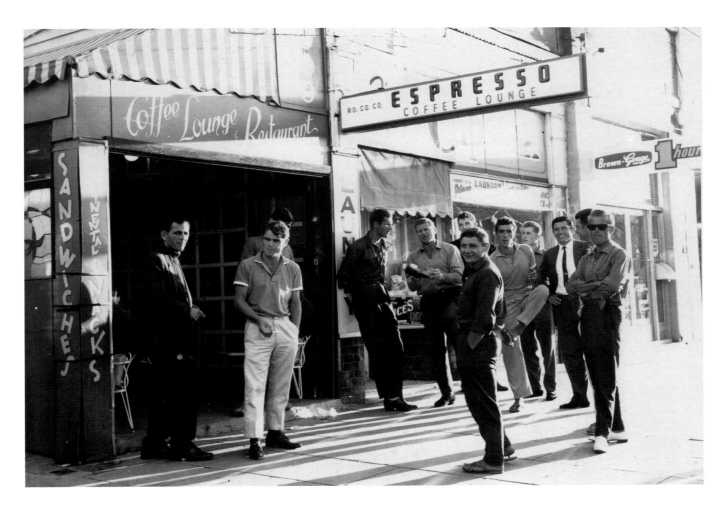

CONTINENTAL AND JEWISH DISHES

Established by Eljasz 'Eddie' Banczewski, the Rococo Coffee Lounge and Restaurant in Fitzroy Street, St Kilda, a bayside Melbourne suburb, catered to Jewish migrants. The menu included popular eastern European Jewish fare, such as potato salad and gefilte fish. Banczewski was born in Białystock, Poland, and in 1939, aged 13, he migrated to Australia with his Polish-Jewish parents. In 1933, when the Nazis seized power in Germany, Australia's Jewish population was 23,000. Despite a hesitancy to increase immigration quotas, by the outbreak of war in 1939 an additional 7,000 to 9,000 Jewish migrants fleeing antisemitism and persecution had arrived in Australia.

PHOTOGRAPHER UNKNOWN, *Outside the Rococo Coffee Lounge and Restaurant*, c. 1960s

JOHN SPOONER (b. 1946), *Al Grassby*, 1986

MULTICULTURALISM

By the 1960s a growing number of migrants and
their supporters were criticising assimilation policies
directed at them and arguing for better services, such
as support for migrant children at schools. They also
sought recognition of their rights, languages and cultural
practices, and of their contribution to Australian society.

Al Grassby, Minister for Immigration (1972–1974) in
the Whitlam Labor government, became one of the
most influential advocates for multiculturalism in
Australia. Eventually, in 1978, the federal government
developed formal multicultural policies based on social
justice principles.

In 1987 the Hawke Labor government created the
Office of Multicultural Affairs within the Department of
Immigration and Ethnic Affairs. After sustained lobbying
from ethnic communities, it was moved to the Prime
Minister's Department, which gave multicultural issues
the same status as women's affairs and Aboriginal
issues. The new office shifted the focus of multicultural
policy from welfare and culture to an emphasis on
the economic benefits of a culturally diverse society.
However, in 1996 it was closed down, and all funds were
withdrawn from its residual functions when it was moved
to the newly created Department of Immigration and
Multicultural Affairs.

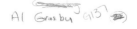

A GREEK FAMILY CELEBRATES EASTER

Easter celebrates the Christian belief in the resurrection of Jesus Christ and is the most significant holiday in the Greek Orthodox Church. In the lead-up to Easter, a period of Lent lasting 40 days is observed with fasting and prayer. This fast is broken on Easter Sunday with a feast and the cracking of red dyed eggs.

In 1975 Melbourne ranked as the fourth most populous 'Greek' city. Today, it is home to the largest population of Greek people living outside of Greece. According to the 2021 Census, a total of 424,744 Australians claim Greek ancestry.

JOHN MCKINNON, *A family celebrates Greek Easter Day in Melbourne by roasting a lamb over a fire in their backyard*, 1975

NICK GIANNOPOULOS (b. 1963);
SIMON PALOMARES (b. 1962); MARIA
PORTESI, *Wogs out of Work*, 1988

WOG HUMOUR

Written by Simon Palomares, Nick
Giannopoulos and Maria Portesi,
the stage production *Wogs out of
Work* debuted at the Melbourne
Comedy Festival in 1987 and ran
for four years. It was succeeded by
the television show *Acropolis Now*
(1989–1992). The word 'wog' was
often used disparagingly to describe
southern European and Middle
Eastern migrants in postwar Australia.
Emerging in the 1980s, so-called
'wog' humour is a form of ethnic
humour created by the children of
postwar migrants. It functions as a
way of reclaiming the word 'wog',
and signalled a shift from previous
representations of migrants that were
inauthentic or stereotypical.

A GIRLS IN PRINT Project
Designed + Printed by
Ethnic Girls Schoolleavers
Project-Fairfield 1983

ETHNIC PRIDE

The Fairfield High School students pictured in this poster are intent on reclaiming the derogatory word 'wog' by declaring pride in their heritage. The title is repeated in Italian, Greek, Hindi, Portuguese, Arabic and Maltese. The poster was created for the Girls in Print Project, run by Amanda Holt and Liz Newell, which produced a series featuring groups of Sydney women. Participants were encouraged to make a poster on an issue relevant to them, such as racism or unemployment. The posters were then distributed to at least 80 schools in New South Wales.

ETHNIC GIRLS SCHOOL-LEAVERS,
We Are Proud to Be Wogs!, 1983

AMANDA HOLT (designer,
active from 1981); JUNO GEMES
(photographer, b. 1944) and ELAINE
PELOT KITCHENER (photographer,
b. 1942), *Tall Ships, Tall Stories*, 1987

RESISTANCE

Celebrations in 1988 marking the bicentenary of the arrival of the First Fleet
prompted a variety of responses. *The Tall Ships, Tall Stories* poster was made
by the Aboriginal Arts Program at Garage Graphix, led by Aboriginal arts
workers in Mount Druitt. It was one of a number of posters which toured in
1988, in an exhibition which critiqued Australia's bicentennial celebrations
and the impact of colonisation upon Aboriginal people.

CELEBRATING THE END OF RAMADAN

Indonesian Muslims gather outside the Marrickville Community Centre in Sydney to mark Eid al-Fitr, the end of Ramadan. Ramadan is observed by Muslims worldwide as a holy month of fasting, reflection and community.

Indonesia is one of Australia's closest neighbours. In the 1996 Census, the Indonesian-born population in Australia numbered 44,177, and by the 2021 Census this had grown to 87,075.

JOHN IMMIG (1935–2018), *Indonesian Muslims gather for the end of Ramadan, Sydney*, 1999

JUNE ORFORD (b. 1946), *Buddhist monks celebrate Vassa at the Thai Buddhist Temple, Box Hill, Victoria*, 2004

VASSA

Buddhist monks at the Thai Buddhist Temple in Melbourne celebrate Vassa (also known as the Rains Retreat or Buddhist Lent) with prayers, meditation and a feast. Once the monks have selected their share of dishes, temple members will join the feast. The retreat coincides with the annual rainy season in Southeast Asia. During this period, the monks will not leave their temple.

Buddhism is the third-largest religious group in Australia. In the 2021 Census, 615,823 Australians identified as Buddhists. Of this group, 59,529 were born in Thailand.

AUSTRALIA'S FASTEST GROWING RELIGION

Hinduism has been present in Australia since the arrival of South Asian labourers and merchants in the nineteenth century. According to the 2021 Census, it recently became Australia's fastest-growing religion, largely owing to increased migrant arrivals from India and Nepal. At the time this photograph was taken 148,100 Australians identified as Hindu, but by 2021 this figure had grown to 684,000.

The *nadaswaram*, a double-reed wind instrument from southern India, is used in temple and marriage rituals to accompany the priests as they chant mantras. The week-long Kumbhabhishekam purification ceremony is performed every 12 years to sanctify the temple and re-energise the devotion of community members.

RODNEY DEKKER (b. 1974), *Two musicians play the nadaswaram at the concluding event of the Kumbhabhishekam, Shri Shiva Vishnu Temple, Carrum Downs, Victoria*, 2007

JOHN IMMIG (1935–2018),
Muslim lifesavers, Cronulla Beach,
New South Wales, 2007

ELIMINATING FEAR

I wanted to prove to people my religion is not a barrier.

A fight between a group of young Middle Eastern men and three volunteer surf lifesavers at North Cronulla Beach on 4 December 2005 led to a race riot on 11 December in which about 5,000 Anglo-Australians violently attacked a group of people of Middle Eastern appearance. As part of efforts to calm racial tensions, a program called 'Same Wave' began to train Muslim lifesavers. Mecca Laalaa, wearing the red and yellow cap, became the first Muslim woman lifesaver in Australia.

'I HEART CABRA'

Cabramatta, or 'Cabra', is one of Sydney's most culturally diverse suburbs. Hosted by Fairfield City Council, the Cabramatta Moon Festival is an annual event that celebrates Sydney's Southeast Asian cultures. The festival showcases a range of cuisines, cultural events and live entertainment.

After staying at migrant hostels in Cabramatta, Villawood, Westbridge or East Hills, many Southeast Asian arrivals in the 1970s and 1980s settled in Cabramatta. In the 2021 Census, 7,995 residents identified as having Vietnamese ancestry, 5,891 as having Chinese ancestry and 1,864 as having Cambodian ancestry.

KEN LEANFORE (b. 1986), *Posing for a selfie in front of a 'I heart Cabra' sign during Fairfield City Council's Cabramatta Moon Festival*, 28 August 2022

SABRINA LAURISTON, *Dance teacher Natalie Toms teaches meke, Fiji's national dance, to (left to right) Tia N, Leilani Qereqeretabua and Kasi K, Bundaberg, Queensland*, 2022

CELEBRATING FIJI DAY

Natalie Toms shares her Fijian culture and heritage with future generations by teaching *meke*, the national dance. Fiji Day is celebrated annually on 10 October, marking the anniversary of both the British Deed of Cession in 1874 and Fijian independence in 1970. Australia is home to the largest Fijian diaspora. The 2021 Census recorded that 68,947 people in Australia were born in Fiji.

LOUISE WHELAN (b. 1967), *Dramyin performers at the Festival of Tibet celebration*, 2010

FESTIVAL OF TIBET

The *dramyin*, a six-string lute, is often used in Tibetan Buddhist religious festivals. The Festival of Tibet was held on 10 July 2010 at Allambie Heights School Community Centre, in Sydney, to mark the 75th birthday of His Holiness the 14th Dalai Lama. The festival was hosted by the Tibetan and Chinese Friendship Society, the Dalai Lama in Australia Limited and the New South Wales Tibetan community.

Tibetan migrants began arriving in Australia in 1973, and by 2010 the community was 900 strong. The Australia Tibet Council estimates that, as of 2020, this number had increased to 2,500.

REFUGEES

Refugees from Vietnam, Laos and Cambodia came to Australia after the Vietnam War ended in 1975, many by boat. Political unrest and conflict in South America and the Middle East also impelled refugees to seek protection in Australia. The suppression of the 'Tiananmen Square' democracy protestors in 1989 saw many Chinese students apply for residency in Australia. The series of wars in the former state of Yugoslavia in the 1990s led to more refugees applying to come. Australia's humanitarian program continues today, with refugees arriving from countries such as Sudan, Eritrea, Somalia, Sri Lanka, Myanmar and Afghanistan.

In the 1970s and 1980s migration became the focus of fierce political debate in Australia. Both Labor and Coalition governments shifted the focus away from assisted migration to schemes specifically designed to attract skilled migrants to fill labour and skill shortages. In 1989, after an eight-year gap, boats carrying asylum seekers began to arrive again. The government responded by introducing mandatory deportation of illegal immigrants, followed in 1992 by mandatory detention of any asylum seekers arriving by boat.

MICHAEL JENSEN (b.1943), *Three girls in cabin on the boat from Vietnam, Darwin*, 1977

COMPASSION AND CONTROL

On Monday 21 November 1977 six small wooden fishing boats carrying 218 Vietnamese men, women and children arrived in Darwin. All were given temporary entry permits into Australia for one month while their future was considered. Immigration Minister Michael MacKellar alluded to the Australian Government's dilemma when he stated, 'We have to combine humanity and compassion with prudent control of unauthorised entry'. Between 1976 and 1986, approximately 94,000 refugees from Laos, Cambodia and Vietnam settled in Australia with about 2,000 arriving by boat. In the 2021 Census more than 330,000 people stated that their ancestry was Vietnamese.

MICHAEL JENSEN (b. 1943),
Vietnamese boat people, Darwin,
1977

LOUISE WHELAN (b. 1967), *Woman protesting in remembrance of the 3,000 Chileans killed on 11 September 1973, Druitt St, Sydney*, 2003

11 DE SEPTIEMBRE

On 11 September 1973 General Augusto Pinochet staged a coup d'état in Chile that led to the overthrow of President Salvador Allende's democratically elected socialist government. Australian bipartisan support to accept Chilean refugees marked a shift from previous immigration programs, which tended to support refugees fleeing communist governments. Between 1974 and 1981 around 6,000 Chileans were admitted to Australia. Pinochet's military dictatorship lasted until 1990. By 1991 Australia's Chilean-born population was more than 24,000.

EVACUATE AND RETURN

In 1999, under Operation Spitfire, around 1,900 East Timorese were evacuated to Australia. Refugees were provided with temporary protection and housed at army barracks, such as East Hills Barracks in Sydney, under the legislative policy named Operation Safe Haven. Safe Haven aimed to provide services to East Timorese residents following attacks on civilians by pro-Indonesia militia groups in May 1999. Violence intensified after the 30 August referendum, in which East Timor voted for independence from Indonesia. As a result, the International Force East Timor (INTERFET), organised and led by Australia, was deployed to restore peace and security in the region. Aided by INTERFET's Australian peacekeepers, refugees began returning to East Timor from December 1999.

DAVID DARE PARKER (b. 1958),
*East Timorese refugees return home,
Dili, East Timor*, 1999

JOHN IMMIG (1935–2018),
*Kosovar refugees with a flag and
map of Kosovo, Singleton, New South
Wales*, 1999

OPERATION SAFE HAVEN

Under Operation Safe Haven, 4,000 ethnic Albanians fleeing conflict in
Kosovo were offered temporary protection in Australia. Refugees were
housed in army bases such as the Lone Pine Barracks in Singleton, north of
Sydney. After the UNHCR declared Kosovo safe again in July 1999, many
Albanians returned home—not all of them voluntarily. By March 2000 there
were fewer than 500 Albanians evacuated under Operation Safe Haven left
in Australia.

KABUL TO MELBOURNE

A group of Afghan refugees arrived in Australia after the Soviet Union's invasion of Afghanistan in 1979. By the early 1990s Australia's Afghan-born population had grown to around 1,000. The Mohmand family left Kabul in 1988 and spent 15 years in Pakistan before coming to Melbourne as refugees.

The Taliban assumed power in 1996, after a period of factional fighting that followed the Soviet withdrawal in 1989. According to the 2021 Census, 41.1 per cent of Australia's Afghan-born population arrived between 1991 and 2010.

JUNE ORFORD (b. 1946), *Fatah and Makai Mohmand displaying a carpet depicting Afghanistan, one of the few personal possessions brought with them*, 2005

LEFT: TONY REDDROP (b. 1961), *Protestors pull down a barbed-wire fence during a protest at the Woomera Detention Centre*, 2002

RIGHT: TONY REDDROP (b. 1961), *Detainees raise a makeshift cross above a barbed-wire fence at the Woomera Detention Centre*, 2002

PROTESTS AT WOOMERA

Over the Easter long weekend in 2002, a crowd of 1,000 gathered outside the Woomera Detention Centre, located in the South Australian desert, to protest the mandatory detention of asylum seekers. Aided by protestors, 50 detainees scaled the 5-metre-tall barbed-wire fence and escaped the facility.

Woomera Detention Centre was part of an official government response to increased unauthorised boat arrivals. Between July 1999 and June 2001 there were 8,316 unauthorised arrivals, compared with 4,114 between 1989 and 1999. Although the centre, which operated from 1999 to 2003, was designed for just 400 people, 1,500 people were detained there at its peak. Most came from Afghanistan, Iran or Iraq.

A TRADITIONAL SKILL IN A NEW LAND

Kwirina lives in Blacktown, New South Wales. She practises the art form of basket weaving, which is traditionally passed down from mother to daughter. The Holroyd Burundi Women's Association received permission from Blacktown City Council to cut papyrus grass in Toongabbie for basket weaving.

In 1993 Burundi's first democratically elected Hutu president was assassinated, triggering over a decade of conflict between Hutu and Tutsi ethnic groups. Around 200,000 people died, and hundreds of thousands more were displaced. Kwirina migrated to Australia with her family in 2004, having spent eight years in a Tanzanian refugee camp.

LOUISE WHELAN (b. 1967), *Kwirina weaving baskets in her Blacktown home*, 2010

CONOR ASHLEIGH (b. 1987),
*Members of Australia's South
Sudanese community gather
for independence celebrations,
Blacktown*, 2014

CELEBRATING INDEPENDENCE

South Sudan gained its independence from the Republic of Sudan on 9 July
2011, following a referendum held earlier that year. In 2014 the South Sudanese
community in Blacktown celebrated the third anniversary of this event. Many
also used the occasion to grieve those killed in the South Sudanese Civil War,
which broke out in 2013. Community leaders have estimated that more than
20,000 people in Australia identify as South Sudanese.

MAHMOUD SALAMEH (b. 1972),
Refugees, 2014

'I RESPECT CARTOONS AND THEY RESPECT ME TOO'

When we arrived by boat, we were 10 Palestinians, 9 refugees from Iraq and me from Syria. The fact that I'm an artist, a political cartoonist, constituted a very good reason, so that I was granted protection.

Mahmoud Salameh grew up in Yamouk camp in Damascus as the child of Palestinian refugees. He arrived in Australia in 2012 and is now a citizen. He had worked as a professional artist in Syria and Lebanon. Since coming to Australia he has continued to create cartoons and animations. Over 15,000 Australians stated they had Palestinian ancestry in the 2021 Census.

ANNE ZAHALKA (b. 1957), *Australia, Isle of Refuge*, 2010

A CHANGING WORLD

A golfer stands on a cliff swinging a golf club, while in the background a refugee boat can be seen approaching the shore. Zahalka's photographic series titled *Homeground!* is a contemporary take on the Resch's, Toohey's and Tooth's beer advertising posters, which idealised Australian sport and leisure and adorned New South Wales pubs and hotels over many decades.

Text within the poster:

HAVING LOST ACCESS TO THEIR TRADITIONAL WATERS, MANY
INDONESIAN FISHERMEN TURN TO PEOPLE SMUGGLING TO SURVIVE
OF OVER 400 MEN ARRESTED FOR PEOPLE SMUGGLING
ONLY 4 HAVE BEEN ORGANISERS OF CRIMINAL SYNDICATES
ALL FACE A MANDATORY SENTENCE OF 5 YEARS IF CONVICTED

THE
SMUGGLER
A BRIDGE OVER TROUBLED BORDERS

WE DON'T CROSS BORDERS: BORDERS CROSS US
www.crossbordersydney.org

DEBORAH KELLY (b. 1962); KATIE
HEPWORTH, *The Smuggler: A Bridge
over Troubled Borders*, 2012

FROM FISHING TO SMUGGLING

In the Arafura Sea, Australia
holds rights to the seabed, while
Indonesia retains rights to the
waters above. This poster was
inspired by Musilmin, an Indonesian
fisherman whose boat was found
in this borderland. In 2009 he was
tried and convicted in Darwin for
illegal fishing. Despite being found
innocent, he was not compensated
for the loss of his boat and resorted
to people smuggling to make a living.
Other fishermen did likewise after
they lost access to their traditional
waters, and the zone of undisputed
water available to them was
overfished. When this poster was
created in 2012, Musilmin had been
convicted of people smuggling and
jailed in Queensland.

SAAD TLAA (b. 1969); ANTHEA
FITZGERALD (b. 1948), *Memorial to
Josefa Rauluni*, 2012

REMEMBERING JOSEFA

Josefa Rauluni, a Fijian national,
jumped to his death from an upstairs
balcony at the Villawood Detention
centre on 20 September 2010. At the
time, Rauluni was facing deportation
having been refused asylum in
Australia. He was an advocate for
democratic change in Fiji and feared
persecution by the military regime if
he returned home. Saad Tlaa, who
was incarcerated at Villawood at the
time, painted a portrait of Rauluni and
had it signed by Villawood residents.
It was presented as a gift to Rauluni's
family. Tlaa's art was used by Anthea
Fitzgerald to design this poster for
the Cross Border Collective.

*Exemption Certificate issued by the NSW Government until the 1970s *Original Nation passport issued by Victorian Elder Robert Thorpe

NEVER CEDED

In 2010 Victorian Elder Robbie Thorpe, a Krautungalung man of the Gunnai Nation, and others issued 'Original Nation passports' to 200 Tamil refugees stranded at sea between Indonesia and Australia. The purpose of the Original Nation passport was to question the Australian Government's right to decide who could cross national borders, because Indigenous sovereignty had never been ceded. The poster features reproductions of an Original Nation passport and one of the Certificates of Exemption issued by the New South Wales Government from 1943 to the 1970s which gave Aboriginal people access to benefits previously denied to them, such as pensions, public education and housing.

ANTHEA FITZGERALD (b. 1948), *Not Y/our Place*, 2012

GUIDE TO THE LIBRARY'S COLLECTIONS

The books, newspapers, documents, letters, paintings, drawings and photographs held by the National Library of Australia provide a storehouse of Australia's migration memories.

CONVICTS

The Library holds an extensive collection of material relating to the administration of the colonies and the convict system. This includes First Fleet journals, drawings, paintings and photographs of convict life, and official documents; for example, *Convict pardon for John Norcup* (1849). Colonial governors had the power to issue tickets of leave and pardons, which allowed convicts varying degrees of freedom. Emancipated convicts could receive a land grant, purchase land and start businesses. Other convicts, who were not serving a life sentence, could gain these freedoms by completing their sentence.

MIGRANT DIARIES AND JOURNALS

Migrant diaries describe what life was like onboard, in the ports stopped at en route. They sometimes convey their first impressions of Australia, as W.J. Douglas did in his 1892 diary, which he later sent back to his brother in Scotland. Douglas wrote of landing in Western Australia and of his travels from Melbourne to Ballarat, and described the local flora and fauna, Australian art and the Australian political system. He also included samples of dried native plant leaves and newspaper cuttings of city scenes and buildings.

MIGRATION DEBATES

Over the last 200 years of Australia's migration history, governments, lobby groups, companies and individuals have all sought to influence public opinion about migration. This is reflected in a large variety of publications promoting migration, providing information for prospective migrants or arguing for changes to Australia's migration policy. These range from nineteenth-century emigrant manuals, such as William Henry Giles Kingston's *Emigrant Manuals No. 1: The British Colonies Described, with Advice to Those Who Cannot Obtain Employment at Home*, published in London in 1851, to twentieth-century guides to Australia's history, primary industries, economy and cities, such as *Australië ... beeld van een natie* (Australia: Image of a nation), a Dutch-language booklet produced by the Department of Immigration in 1959.

Government ministers, such as Arthur Calwell, Australia's first immigration minister, produced pamphlets intended to explain migration schemes to the general public. In publications such as the pamphlet *I Stand by White Australia*, published in 1949, Calwell reiterated the White Australia policy. Non-government organisations also published pamphlets outlining their position on this policy; for example, the Immigration Reform Group, established by students and academics at the University of Melbourne in 1960, campaigned for the policy's reform. It produced *Control or Colour Bar? A Proposal for Change in Australia's*

Immigration Policy, which stressed the economic benefits of migration and highlighted the damage done to Australia's reputation by the White Australia policy.

Sometimes migrants produced their own publications; for example, Wong Loy-Wong (aka Samuel Wong) published *Arrogant White Australia: The Case for a Quota for Coloured Migrants* in 1949:

> This White Australia Question leads us to a very illogical and strange conclusion, because according to missionary propaganda in Asia we are told that we, the people in Asia, are good enough to enter the Pearly Gate[s] ... but not good enough to live a short life on the Australian continent with Messers Chifley, Menzies, Calwell, Fadden and their followers.

MIGRATION STORIES

Besides arguing for better rights and against discrimination, migrants have published their own memoirs and fiction about their experiences. In his book *The Happiest Refugee* (2010), which was reworked as a children's book *The Little Refugee* in 2011, the well-known comedian and artist Anh Do relates how his family left Vietnam on an overcrowded boat and describes the challenges they faced when settling in Australia.

Other books written by migrants record contact with First Nations people. An example is *Galtjintana-Pepa: Kristianirberaka Mbontala* (1891), the first Aranda book of Christian instruction and worship. It was compiled by Friedrich Adolf Hermann Kempe, a German Lutheran missionary who arrived in South Australia in 1875 and who was one of the founders of Hermannsburg Mission in Central Australia. A more recent work, Samia Khatun's *Australianama: The South Asian Odyssey in Australia* (2018), traces a history of Muslims in Australia through Sufi poetry, Urdu travel tales, Persian dream texts and Arabic concepts, as well as Wangkangurru song-poetry, Arabunna women's stories and Kuyani histories. Khatun argues that Aboriginal and South Asian language sources can transform our understanding of the past, present and future.

PHOTOGRAPHS

Since the introduction of the daguerreotype to Sydney in the 1840s, migrants have used photography to document their experiences, their families and their new homes in Australia. Some of these photographs were sent to family still living in the homeland, as a reminder to loved ones left behind, while others remained here in Australia. In this way, photographs, sometimes accompanied by letters, became a bridge to connect people over distance and time: for example, Alberto Rizzo, building a new home in Sydney, and his mother, still in Italy.

Other images tell familial migration stories from across the generational divide. William Yang and Anna Zhu have both used photography to reveal their ancestors' experience of being migrants. Yang's *Australian Chinese* (2001) and *My Uncle's Murder* (2009) explore stories of his grandparents, who migrated in the late nineteenth century, his family's desire to assimilate in order to be accepted and his desire that surfaced in his mid-30s to reclaim his Chinese culture. Zhu's *Yah Yah* (2008) photographic series touches on the theme of the sense of isolation sometimes experienced by migrants, especially those who left their homelands at an advanced age.

ALBERTO RIZZO (1917–1985), *The home Alberto Rizzo built with his family on Clarence Street, Merrylands, in Western Sydney, seen here in the final stages of construction*, c. 1960

GOVERNMENT DOCUMENTS

The Library's manuscript collections demonstrate government decision-making and democratic processes. They include the papers of government officials, such as John Tolson Massey, who was the Commonwealth coordinator of the Good Neighbour Movement (1949–1959), which aimed to integrate new migrants by promoting rapid assimilation, as well as those of government ministers.

Not only do these collections contain correspondence, notes and letters written by members of the general public, they also contain reports, advertisements and other documents relating to the administration of migration and settlement programs. The New Settlers' League of Australia (Queensland Division) leaflet *'Family Plan': Together as Friends* (c. 1949–1950) is one such document. The New Settlers' League of Australia was established by the federal government in 1921, in partnership with the states and civic-minded volunteers. The league aimed to promote immigration and assist new immigrants by welcoming new settlers, assisting them to secure employment, offering advice and promoting their welfare and settlement.

NEWSPAPERS

Non–English language newspapers, produced by, and for, migrant communities and their descendants, are valuable sources of information in their own right. These papers enable people to keep up to date with news from their places of origin and learn about their new country. They are produced in a range of languages and cater to an audience who understand varying levels of English.

One of the longest-running ethnic media publications in Australia is the Sydney-based newspaper *Le Courrier Australien* (*The Australian Mail*), published between 1892 and 2011. In 2016 the paper was relaunched as a website in both French and English. *Le Courrier Australien* is credited with helping to integrate the French-speaking

PHOTOGRAPHER UNKNOWN, *Ethnic newspapers are prominent on this kiosk in Elizabeth Street, Melbourne*, 1991

community in Australia, while exposing the broader Australian public to French culture and politics. Issues of the print newspaper have been digitised and can be read via Trove.

MUSICAL WORKS

Music is another form of self-expression that can provide a personal record of history and culture. The Library's oral history collection includes recordings of folk music performed by migrants and refugees. These can be found in collections such as the Salvatore Rossano folklore collection, the Rob and Olya Willis folklore collection and the Alex Hood folklore collection. In particular, the Library is home to a large collection of Maltese folk music performed by *ghannejia* (folk singers, pronounced 'arn-ay-uh') in Australia.

I want to tell you of our adventure
And I hope that I don't err
Whatever I say to you is real
And it happened to me, and to my husband and to
our children as well.

These lyrics were written and sung in Maltese by Georgina Camenzuli. In 1997 Kevin Bradley and Barry York interviewed Georgina and her husband, Nazzareno, for the Maltese-Australian folklife and social history project. The Camenzulis provided an account of their voyage to Australia in 1958 on the MS *Skaubryn*, which sank in the Indian Ocean after a fire broke out in the engine room. Georgina wrote her *għana* (fact-based ballad, pronounced 'anah') 'Saga of the *Skaubryn* Migrants' while doing laundry at home. The lyrics share the couple's experiences on the sinking vessel, their rescue and arrival in Australia.

ORAL HISTORY INTERVIEWS

The National Library's Oral History and Folklore Collection began in the 1950s and now comprises more than 55,000 hours of recordings. Australians from diverse backgrounds are featured in this collection. Migrants and refugees describe their journeys via plane, ship or fishing boat. They explain how they adapted to a new culture, while keeping their own traditions alive. Second and subsequent generations also explain their experiences. They also express feelings of loneliness and belonging, and explain how migration has shaped their identity.

LEIGH HENNINGHAM (b. 1960), *Portrait of Everest Pitt*, 2022

Everest Pitt, for example, was interviewed for the Fijian-Australian oral history project in 2022. One of 60 people interviewed for this collection, she describes her upbringing in Fiji, her arrival in Australia ('So I arrived as a 21-year-old. I actually celebrated my 21st birthday here in 1974') and discusses her identity as a Fijian-Australian 48 years after migrating.

FAMILY HISTORY

As historical records have become more accessible, family history research has risen in popularity. The Library offers a range of resources, such as newspapers, electoral rolls and shipping records, that the Australian family historian will find useful. These can be accessed online, or in the Newspapers and Family History zone of the Main Reading Room. Research materials from a variety of partners around Australia are also available on Trove.

OUR COLLECTING

The National Library of Australia continues to collect material relating to Australia's migration history. The Library works with culturally and linguistically diverse communities to create a record of their experiences in Australia. Targeted collecting projects with Chinese- and Fijian-Australians between 2021 and 2023 have increased the representation of these communities in the collection.

A broad range of material is collected, including newspapers and oral history interviews. These resources are freely available for all to use when researching their own migrant family histories.

More information about the Library's collections is available on Trove and through the Library's catalogue. Visit us online or in Canberra.

IMAGE CREDITS

Australian Agricultural Company (issuer)
Australian Agricultural Company share certificate 1825
nla.cat-vn1132461

George French Angas (artist, 1822–1886); **James W. Giles** (lithographer, 1801–1870)
Klemsic [Klemzig], a village of German settlers near Adelaide
from *South Australia Illustrated*
London: Thomas McLean, 1847
hand-coloured lithograph
nla.cat-vn324029

Samuel Thomas Gill (1818–1880)
Pennys Stopes, B.B. [Burra Burra] Mine, 12 April 1847 1847
watercolour
nla.cat-vn1981348

Edwin Stocqueler (1829–1895)
Australian gold diggings c. 1855
oil on canvas
Rex Nan Kivell Collection
National Library of Australia and National Gallery of Australia
nla.cat-vn1861686

Nicholas Chevalier (artist, 1828–1902); **Frederick Grosse** (engraver, 1828–1894)
Chinese people ground-sluicing, near Beechworth, Victoria 1867
wood engraving print
nla.cat-vn422267

Yackaduna (aka Tommy McRae) (c. 1835–1901)
Aboriginal man and Chinese man, and Aboriginal men fighting 1881
from *Sketchbook of Aboriginal Daily Life Scenes, Wahgunyah Region, Victoria*
nla.cat-vn6296671

John Flynn (1880–1951)
An 'Afghan' camel driver with two unknown men, standing next to a camel train c. 1912–1930
Australian Inland Mission Collection
nla.cat-vn2171143

Thomas Griffith Taylor (1880–1963)
The New Oxford Wall Maps of Australia
London: Oxford University Press by George Philip & Son, c. 1920
nla.cat-vn6098381

Albert Lomer and Co.
Recruiters and boat's crew, New Hebrides, Queensland labour traffic c. 1890
albumen silver print
nla.cat-vn1865796

Kwong Sue Duk (1853–1929)
Account book c. 1913–1920s
ink on paper
Papers of the Kwong family, 1891–2001
nla.cat-vn3006822

Maker unknown
Christening gown first worn by Kwong Mui Ying (May), and later by other members of Kwong Sue Duk's family 1901
Papers of the Kwong family, 1891–2001
nla.cat-vn3006822

Photographer unknown
Kwong Mui Ying (May), first daughter of Kwong Sue Duk's fourth wife, Wong Kwei Far 1918
Papers of the Kwong family, 1891–2001
nla.cat-vn3006822

Photographer unknown
Anthony Wehby, Braidwood, Victoria c. 1912
Records of the Australian Lebanese Historical Society, 1890–2015
nla.cat-vn6929220

English-to-Arabic Dictionary, carried by Anthony George Wehby 1910
print and ink on paper
Records of the Australian Lebanese Historical Society, 1890–2015
nla.cat-vn6929220

Invoice and order form from Stanton Melick, Warehousemen & Manufacturers, Redfern, to Mr A.G. Wehby, Braidwood 12 May 1931
print and ink on paper
Records of the Australian Lebanese Historical Society, 1890–2015
nla.cat-vn6929220

Marie Bashir's school report card for grade 3 c. 1930
print and ink on paper
Records of the Australian Lebanese Historical Society, 1890–2015
nla.cat-vn6929220

John Flynn (1880–1951)
Japanese pearl divers, Broome, Western Australia c. 1914
Australian Inland Mission Collection
nla.cat-vn654526

William Emanuel Naunton (words and music, 1871–1939); **Harry John Willmott Gyles** (words, 1880–1959)
White Australia: The Great National Policy Song
Melbourne: A.M. Dinsdale, 1910
nla.cat-vn6977121

Maker unknown
The Flow of Population 1920
nla.cat-vn7089362

Photographer unknown
A Chinese-Australian in his market garden, Northern Territory c. 1930
nla.cat-vn4612294

Photographer unknown
Seamen's Union General Secretary Tom Walsh (centre, with his wife, Adela Pankhurst Walsh, at his left) and Assistant Secretary Jacob Johnson on their way to their deportation hearing at Darlinghurst Courthouse, Sydney
3 September 1925
nla.cat-vn6303306

Theodor Engel (1886–1978)
Study of Professor Mayer, a Dunera Boy, at Tatura, Victoria 1942
pencil on paper
Portraits of Dunera Boys, 1941–1943
nla.cat-vn6258914

Theodor Engel (1886–1978)
Watercolour of Hay Internment Camp
watercolour
Records of Hay Internment Camp, 1940–1941
nla.cat-vn2921273

James Northfield (illustrator, 1887–1973); **Commonwealth Immigration Office** (issuer)
The Land of Opportunity: Australia's Irrigation Enterprises
Melbourne: Queen City Printers, 1924
nla.cat-vn8688888

Charles Dixon *(1872–1934)*
By P&O to Australia: Fortnightly Sailings from London and Marseilles: Australasia, Egypt, India, Ceylon, Straits, China, Japan, via Egypt and Ceylon
London: The Lamson Agency, Philip Reed, 1928
lithograph
nla.obj-2632150972

The Intelligence and Tourist Bureau
South Australia for the Fruit Grower
Adelaide: R.E.E. Rodgers, Government Printer, c. 1919
nla.cat-vn920050

Commonwealth Immigration Office
Tropical Agriculture in Australia
Melbourne: Albert J. Mullett, Government Printer, c. 1921
nla.cat-vn2150170

Minister for External Affairs
Australia: The Land of Sunshine Health & Prosperity
Melbourne: Syd Day the Printer, c. 1915
nla.cat-vn6608980

Commonwealth Immigration Office (1920–1927)
Australia's Offer to the British Boy
Melbourne: Albert J. Mullett, Government Printer, 1922
nla.cat-vn1253148

Commonwealth Immigration Office (1920–1927)
Australia Invites the British Domestic Girl
Melbourne: Albert J. Mullett, Government Printer, 1924
nla.cat-vn8675424

Photographer unknown
Protest against treatment of British soldier-settlers outside Australia House, London 1938
nla.cat-vn3117901

John Mulligan (1927–1996)
Teenage and child immigrants from Great Britain brought out by Dr Barnardo's on the P&O liner Canberra 10 October 1963
nla.cat-vn2344009

Artist unknown
Program presented to the Honourable Arthur Calwell, Minister for Immigration 1949
pen, ink, watercolour on paper
nla.cat-vn3670758

Arthur Calwell (1896–1973)
20,000,000 Australians in Our Time! Statement of Immigration Policy by the Minister for Immigration, the Hon. Arthur A. Calwell, to the House of Representatives
Melbourne: Department of immigration, 8 September 1949
nla.cat-vn97797

Photographer unknown
The Gamboa family reunited in Australia 1952
Papers of the Gamboa family, 1949–1999
nla.cat-vn997866

Photographer unknown
Verners and Girts Linde with their mural for the arts and craft exhibition at the Australian Citizenship Convention 1950
nla.cat-vn3695366

The New Australians' Cultural Association
Testimonials presented to the people of Australia and the government by European migrants to Australia, on the occasion of the Australian Citizenship Convention, Canberra 1953
ink, paint, gold leaf on parchment in a leather-bound volume
nla.cat-vn1822125

Boriska Frankovits' French identity document 1951
Yellow Star of David badge worn by Marcel Frankovits 1940–1944
cotton
Ford employee badge belonging to Thomas Frankovits c. 1950
Thomas Frankovits' driver's licence 1948
Papers of André Frankovits, 1889–2013
nla.cat-vn6857235

Artist unknown
£10 Takes You to Australia: Children under 19 Go Free!
London: Australia House, c. 1960
nla.cat-vn8039878

Artist unknown
Australia: Lloyd Triestino: MN Australia, MN Oceania, MN Neptunia
Milan: Amilcare Pizzi SA, c. 1957–1963
nla.cat-vn3726199

Joe Greenberg (1923–2007)
Australia: Land of Tomorrow
Canberra: Commonwealth Department of Information, c. 1948
nla.cat-vn3682938

'W.P.' and Joe Greenberg (1923–2007)
There's a Man's Job for You in Australia
Canberra: Commonwealth Department of Information, c. 1947
nla.cat-vn3279439

Wolfgang Sievers (1913–2007)
Tunnel work at T-2, Snowy Mountains Hydro-electric Scheme 1957
gelatin silver print
Wolfgang Sievers Photographic Archive
nla.cat-vn4801856

Central Office of Information, Great Britain
The Colombo Plan
London: Curwen Press Ltd, 1969
nla.cat-vn1768860

Ern McQuillan (1926–2018)
Turkish migrants in the dining hall of the Villawood Migrant Hostel, Sydney 1968
reproduction from negative
nla.cat-vn5983214

Photographer unknown
Outside the Rococo Coffee Lounge and Restaurant
Papers relating to Rococo Coffee Lounge and Restaurant, St Kilda, c. 1960s
nla.cat-vn8613883

John Spooner (b. 1946)
Al Grassby 1986
pen, ink and brush on paper
nla.cat-vn360540

John McKinnon
A family celebrates Greek Easter Day in Melbourne by roasting a lamb over a fire in their backyard 1975
nla.cat-vn4977650

Nick Giannopoulos (b. 1963); Simon Palomares (b. 1962); Maria Portesi
Wogs out of Work 1988
theatre program
nla.cat-vn3532232

Ethnic Girls School-leavers
We Are Proud to Be Wogs!
Fairfield, NSW: Girls in Print Project, 1983
nla.cat-vn5016725

Amanda Holt (designer, active from 1981); Juno Gemes (photographer, b. 1944) and Elaine Pelot Kitchener (photographer, b. 1942)
Tall Ships, Tall Stories 1987
nla.cat-vn8418095

John Immig (1935–2018)
Indonesian Muslims gather for the end of Ramadan, Sydney 1999
nla.cat-vn3093617

June Orford (b. 1946)
Buddhist monks celebrate Vassa at the Thai Buddhist Temple, Box Hill, Victoria 2004
digital photograph
nla.cat-vn3312122

Rodney Dekker (b. 1974)
Two musicians play the nadaswaram at the concluding event of the Kumbhabhishekam, Shri Shiva Vishnu Temple, Carrum Downs, Victoria 2007
inkjet print
nla.cat-vn4318916

John Immig (1935–2018)
Muslim lifesavers, Cronulla Beach, New South Wales 2007
Social Documentary Photographs, Sydney 2007–2011
nla.cat-vn6616574

Ken Leanfore (b. 1986)
Posing for a selfie in front of a 'I heart Cabra' sign during Fairfield City Council's Cabramatta Moon Festival
digital photograph
Fairfield City Council's Cabramatta Moon Festival, 28 August 2022
nla.obj-3128830839

Sabrina Lauriston
Dance teacher Natalie Toms teaches meke, Fiji's national dance, to (left to right) Tia N, Leilani Qereqeretabua and Kasi K, Bundaberg, Queensland
digital photograph
Fiji Day Celebrations, Bundaberg, Queensland, 8 October 2022
nla.obj-3123461538

Louise Whelan (b. 1967)
Dramyin performers at the Festival of Tibet celebration 2010
digital photograph
nla.cat-vn5756674

Michael Jensen (b.1943)
Three girls in cabin on the boat from Vietnam, Darwin 1977
nla.cat-vn3209932

Michael Jensen (b. 1943)
Vietnamese boat people, Darwin 1977
nla.cat-vn3209915

Louise Whelan (b. 1967)
Woman protesting in remembrance of the 3,000 Chileans killed on 11 September 1973, Druitt St, Sydney 2003
silver gelatin print
nla.cat-vn3085013

David Dare Parker (b. 1958)
East Timorese refugees return home, Dili, East Timor 1999
archival inkjet print
nla.cat-vn4392875

John Immig (1935–2018)
Kosovar refugees with a flag and map of Kosovo, Singleton, New South Wales 1999
nla.cat-vn3092550

June Orford (b. 1946)
Fatah and Makai Mohmand displaying a carpet depicting Afghanistan, one of the few personal possessions brought with them 2005
digital photograph
nla.cat-vn3536543

Tony Reddrop (b. 1961)
Protestors pull down a barbed-wire fence during a protest at the Woomera Detention Centre 2002
digital type-c print
nla.cat-vn3295939

Tony Reddrop (b. 1961)
Detainees raise a makeshift cross above a barbed-wire fence at the Woomera Detention Centre 2002
digital type-c print
nla.cat-vn3295945

Louise Whelan (b. 1967)
Kwirina weaving baskets in her Blacktown home
digital photograph
Collection of Photographs of Multicultural Communities Living in New South Wales, 2010
nla.cat-vn5756649

Conor Ashleigh (b. 1987)
Members of Australia's South Sudanese community gather for independence celebrations, Blacktown 2014
digital photograph
Australia's South Sudanese Refugee Community, 2010–2015
nla.cat-vn7459976

Mahmoud Salameh (b. 1972)
Refugees 2014
digital print

Anne Zahalka (b. 1957)
Australia, Isle of Refuge 2010
archival pigment ink print
nla.cat-vn5399861

Deborah Kelly (b. 1962); **Katie Hepworth**
The Smuggler: A Bridge over Troubled Borders
Sydney: Cross Border Collective, 2012
nla.cat-vn6452205

Saad Tlaa (b. 1969); **Anthea Fitzgerald** (b. 1948)
Memorial to Josefa Rauluni
Sydney: Cross Border Collective, 2012
nla.cat-vn6452153

Anthea Fitzgerald (b. 1948)
Not Y/our Place
Sydney: Cross Border Collective, 2012
nla.cat-vn6452188

Alberto Rizzo (1917–1985)
The home Alberto Rizzo built with his family on Clarence Street, Merrylands, in Western Sydney, seen here in the final stages of construction c. 1960
Papers of Alberto Rizzo, 1951–1978
nla.cat-vn6937830

Photographer unknown
Ethnic newspapers are prominent on this kiosk in Elizabeth Street, Melbourne 1991
nla.cat-vn1060046

Leigh Henningham (b. 1960)
Portrait of Everest Pitt 2022
nla.cat-vn8685568

Published by National Library of Australia Publishing
Canberra ACT 2600
ISBN: 9781922507648
© National Library of Australia 2024

The National Library of Australia acknowledges Australia's First Nations
Peoples—the First Australians—as the Traditional Owners and Custodians
of this land and gives respect to the Elders—past and present—and through
them to all Australian Aboriginal and Torres Strait Islander people.

First Nations Peoples are advised this book contains depictions and names
of deceased people, and content that may be considered culturally sensitive.

This book contains words and descriptions that reflect the attitudes of the
period in which the item was created and may now be considered offensive.
If you have concerns or queries, please contact Exhibitions.

Publisher: Lauren Smith
Authors: Dr Guy Hansen, Shelly McGuire, Allister Mills, Dr Karen
Schamberger, Nicole Schwirtlich
Managing editor: Amelia Hartney
Editor: Robert Nichols
Designer: Hugh Ford (internals), Nick Williams, Artikel Design (cover)
Image coordinator: Madeleine Warburton
Printed in Australia by CanPrint on FSC®-certified paper.

Find out more about NLA Publishing at nla.gov.au/national-library-publishing.
A catalogue record for this book is available from the National Library of
Australia.